Playground Construction & Dimensions

O.P. Sharma

KHEL SAHITYA KENDRA
7/26, Ansari Road, Darya Ganj, New Delhi-110002
Ph.: (O) 65190343, 42564726, 42564726 (M) 9811088729
(R) 47091605 Fax: 42564726
E-mail: khelsahitya1@rediffmail.com

Published by:

KHEL SAHITYA KENDRA

7/26, Ansari Road, Darya Ganj, New Delhi-110002
Ph.: (O) 65190343, 42564726 (M) 9811088729
(R) 47091605 (Fax) 42564726
E-mail: *khelsahitya1@rediffmail.com*
Website: *www.khelsahitya.trade-india.com*

I.S.B.N. – 81-7524-460-7

PRINTED IN INDIA 2007

Laser Typeset by:

JAIN MEDIA GRAPHICS

C-4/95-A, Keshav Puram, (Lawrence Road),
Delhi-110035. (Mobiles) 9911151534, 9350556511

Printed by:

NEW GYAN OFFSET PRINTERS

Shahjada Bagh, Delhi-110035

[redacted]

CONTENTS

CHAPTER-1

THE SIGNIFICANCE OF PHYSICAL EDUCATION AND THE CONSTRUCTION OF SPORTS FACILITIES

In the life of people, physical education has an important role to play. It involves development in all aspects of life. Physical education and exercises not only improve the health of an individual or give him physical vigour or full working capacity but also pleasure and relaxation. He develops his mental process.

Such people are in the best position to fulfill their objective and serve the nation. Any excellence in sports achieved at international competition also adds to the reputation of the nation.

As such, physical education is indispensable for development of efficiency and skills of an individual for the overall development of his intellectual, social, cultural and economic faculties.

The first requirement for this purpose is to provide adequate facilities for physical education. Sports facilities should be of the highest standard and they should accord with the cultural setting of the country. The sports stadia should be of suitable architectural style. The designs can be simple and modest but at the same time aesthetic and appealing.

First of all importance should be given to the building of small scale or medium scale sport grounds, sports halls and providing proper facilities for practicing physical exercises and play sports and games. The turn of large-scale stadium games come later. It will be futile to build large-scale stadium. when the normal facilities for sports are missing. The big stadium are seldom needed. They are build at a high cost and absorb all the resources at the cost of providing normal small-scale facilities. The normal small-scale facilities can be provided at a relatively much less cost.

It is necessary to provide the normal small-scale facilities at as large a scale as possible so that the whole people can actively participate in games and sports. Not only young men and women should be enthused to take part in sport but even young children and old people should be encouraged to participate. The normal playgrounds should be constructed in every nook and corner of the country where people are interested or made to take interest in games. The importance of games should be brought home to them. Various competitions should be held for all age groups, prizes should be distributed and important people should be invite to these functions. Proper publicity should also be given by the media.

Schools and colleges are the best institutions for inculcating the habit and love for sports, The age, mental and physical alarcity of the students is best suited for this purpose. They should be made to realize the importance of sports. The old idea that it interferes in education should be set aside but it should be brought home to them that this will not only improve their physical health but also their mental, intellectual, social and cultural development and thus can contribute greatly in the development of the nation. They should not be made to forget the great maxim, 'The battle of Walerloo was fought on the playground of Eden.' Sports should find a proper place in the curriculum of schools and college activities.

CHAPTER-2

PRELIMINARY CONSIDERATIONS BEFORE PLANNING SPORTS FACILITIES

Before undertaking actual planning of the sports facilities, it is necessary to pay attention to some important questions. If these are not given due consideration, the work may have to be given up half-way or it may not meet the requirement or fulfill the objectives. The problems are :-

(i) Whether the facilities being provided will be fully used after construction or in distant future.

(ii) Whether there are any rules and regulations which prohibit the provision of sports facilities at the site proposed to be selected.

(iii) Whether the finance for construction is available.

(iv) Whether the area is sufficient to meet the present requirement and for future expansion.

(V) Whether the building material and machinery for construction and workmen are available.

After consideration of these problems, attention has to be paid to the planning and designing of the construction work.

Even for small work, it will be worthwhile to undertake these jobs. These should not be brushed away as a matter of routine. Even small work will be hindered if these considerations are not made. It may result in faulty and uneconomic construction. Many a problem may arise after the work is completed.

Before planning and designing of work, it will be better to visit and examine the existing sport facilities of similar nature. The services of an expert in construction can also be utilized. The standardized structural parts or design documents are available. These should be made use of as these help reduce the cost and period of construction.

The construction work should be sub-divided in two categories that which is needed at present and that which can be taken up later. It will be better to postpone the future requirement to a future date and leave the area unused.

The maintenance cost of the work will be high if it is not constructed properly. At the time of construction, this factor should be kept in mind. So good building material should be used and workmanship should be of high standard.

The sports facilities provided will have to be properly maintained and cared for. These have to be kept in good repair. Skilled workers might have to be kept for the care of ground and equipment. Expenses involved should not be grudged and taken in to account before embarking upon construction.

CHAPTER-3

FUNDAMENTALS IN DESIGNING PLAYING FIELDS AND SPORTS GROUNDS

AREA REQUIRED

In rural areas, provision of space for sports does not pose a problem. Further, people have to exert themselves physically in their work. So they do not hanker after sports. The times have, however, changed and they should be encouraged and whatever facilities are required should be provided.

In small towns or cities, the area required for sports also do not pose a problem. But as the small towns or cities gradually develop, they create a problem if the area for sports required for the population in the foreseeable future is not calculated and er-marked.

In big cities, this really creates difficulties. even if, at the time of planning a city or at the time of its expansion, the area required for sports is calculated and er-marked. But with the rapid increase in population, the calculations may prove to be quite unsatisfactory. Therefore, in calculating areas required for sports, we should err on the right side and have more space than is actually required in the foreseeable future.

The importance of sports have increased due to national, continental and international competitions, huge sums awarded to the winners, publicity given by T.V. and newspapers and respect and dignity a nation gets in winning medals at such events, Considering all this, much area should be left or provided for sports.

The consideration of area is the first task. Thereafter it has to be considered as to where it is required. For instance, a city should be divided in different zones to provide space for sports not far distant from the people requiring these facilities. In densely populated area, there is no way out except to be a little miser in calculating or providing space for sports. In the case of small built up areas, we can afford to be liberal.

Around the sports area, it is necessary to provide some area for greenary. In some populated areas, it is necessary to provide more area for greenary, though it may not always be possible. In loosely knit areas, proper areas for greenary should be left. Normally 1/3 of the area for sports is set apart for this purpose.

In addition, areas for paths, roads, dressing cabins, water-closets, lavatories, parking space for bicycle, scooters and cars, etc. have also to be included. Some times there is a competition, and many people come to see these competitions. So proper area has to be left for seating of the spectators.

The area required for sports facilities per inhabitant should be worked out. This should take in account the interest of the inhabitants in a particular field.

Gross sports ground area 4.5 to 5.5 m^2 per inhabitant as indicated below is required for each inhabitant. This can be increased or decreased according to the interest of the inhabitants.

1. Useful area of sports field 3.0 to 3.5 m^2 per inhabitant (Primary or main field)
2. Children's playground .5 m^2 per inhabitant
3. Green and various athletic and smaller sports facilities (Secondary facilities)

1.0 to 1.5 m^2 per inhabitant

4.5 to 5.5 m^2 per inhabitant

Further, a Gymnasium area of 0.07 m^2 perinhabitant and an open air swimming pool area of 1.0 m^2 per inhabitant are required.

Different types of sports grounds may be necessary at different places according to requirement. Illustrations of four types of sports ground - simple sports ground, sports ground including track and subsidiary facilities, sports park with subsidary fields and sports park with small stadium, are given below.

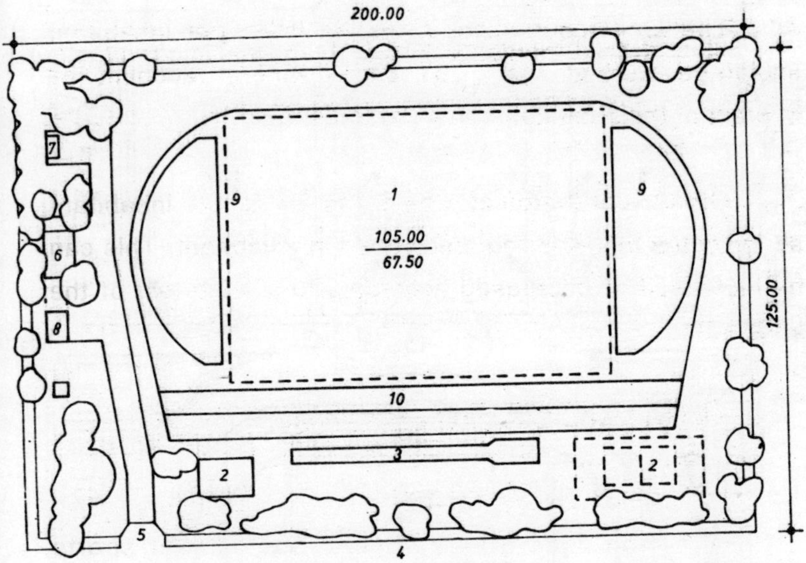

Simple sports ground

1 Playing field
2 Volleyball fields
3 Broad-jump facility
4 Approach road
5 Entrance
6 Dressing room
7 Water-closets
8 Bicycle stand
9 Connection for lawn-sprinkler
10 Track

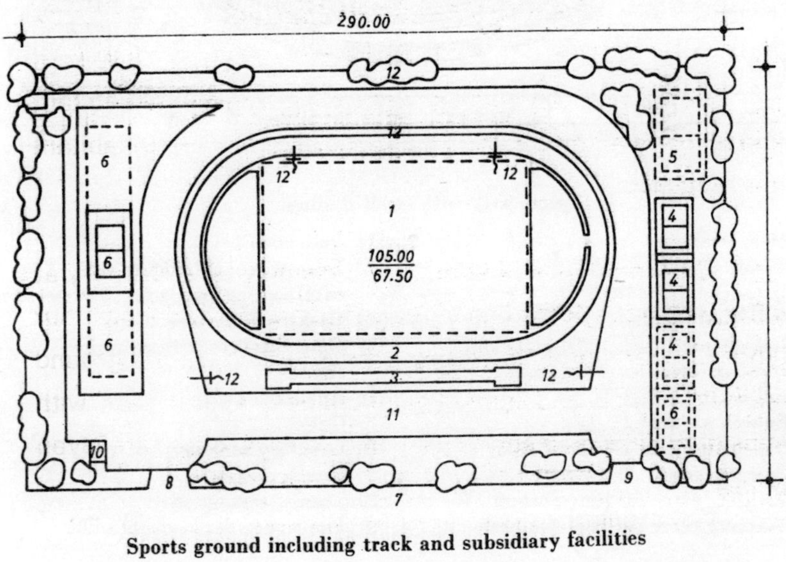

Sports ground including track and subsidiary facilities

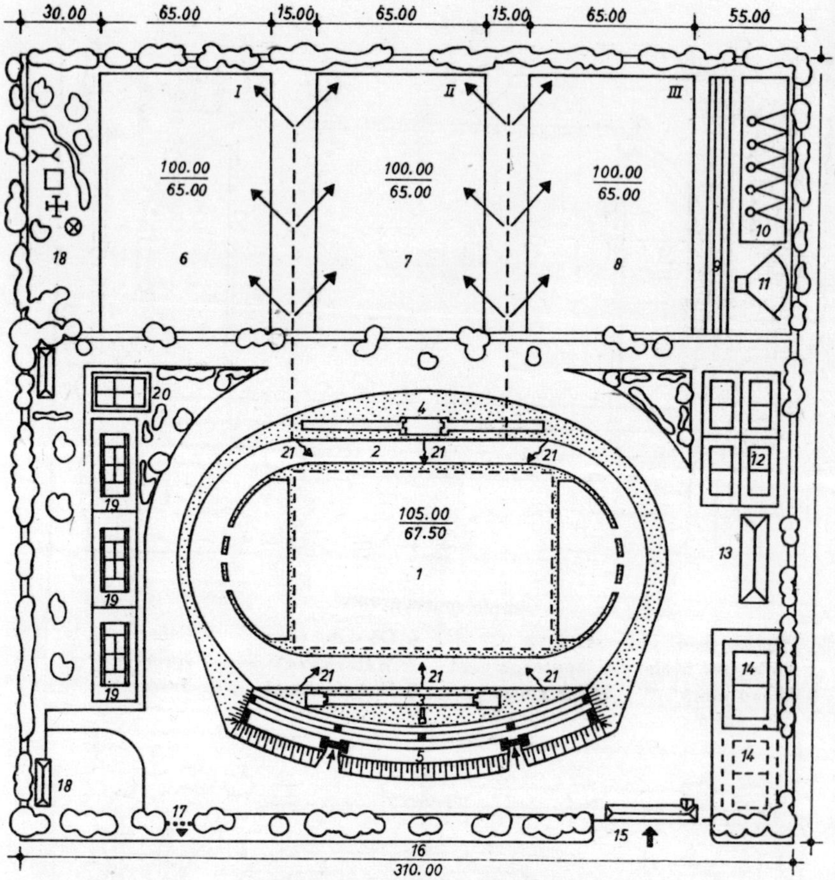

Sports park with small stadium

1 Main field
2 Track
3 Broad-jump facility
4 Pole-vault facility
5 Grand stand with 1,000 seats and standing-room for 400 persons
6 Subsidiary field I
7 Subsidiary field II
8 Subsidiary field III (hard field)
9 Training track
10 Training place for shot-putters
11 Training place for high-jumpers
12 Volleyball fields
13 Dressing-room building with entrance for sportsmen and women
14 Basketball playing courts
15 Main entrance with entrance structure
16 Approach road
17 Outlet
18 Lavatory building
19 Tennis courts
20 Tennis training court
21 Connection for lawn-sprinkler

Inhabitants of village or town (ward)	Central sports facility	School sports facilities	Children's play-grounds	Gross sports ground area	Halls
2,000 to 3,000	Sports field with secondary facilities 2.5 ha	Central sports facility used	-----	2.5 ha	1
6,000 to 8,000	Sports field with secondary facilities and track 4.5 ha	Central sports facility used	700 m2	4.72 ha	1 to 2
up to 15,000	Sports park including various playing fields and stand 8.0 ha	0.8 ha	1,400 m2	8.94 ha	2 to 3
up to 50,000	Sports park with small stadium 11.0 ha	according to number of schools, 5 to 8 ha	1.5 ha	25 to 28 ha	1 large hall for indoor games; 10 to 12 gymnasia

These are required in accordance with the population of a town.

Indoor swimming pools are also required to be provided. In small towns, swimming pools for teaching swimming to children are provided. In a big town, in addition to this facilities, swimming pools are provided by clubs, hotels and sport authorities.

Special sports facilities for water sports, riding, polo motoring, etc. are also required. These have not been included in the areas worked out. Extra areas for such sports, wherever necessary, will have to be included.

LOCATION

Due consideration should be given to the location of a sports ground. Normally a compromise is made in selecting the area on account of economical, functional, constructional and architectural requirements. As no change can be made later on or if a change is made, it will involve great expense, greatest care should be taken in selecting the site.

In selecting the site, attention has to be paid to the traffic requirements, geographical factors, nature of the soil and aesthetical and structural considerations.

TRAFFIC REQUIREMENTS

Sports facilities should be within easy reach of the people intending to use these facilities. This will increase the number of participants.

The play ground for children should be within residential areas. It should be ensured that they do not have to walk much distance and they have not to cross main road. Therefore, in big cities and towns where there is much traffic, a large number of playing fields will have to be provided.

In schools, the sports facilities should be provided at a little distance from the school building so as not to allow the noise in sports to interfere with studies. Trees can also be planted within the school building and sports ground to curb the noise. Enough area should be left for sport ground and all necessary considerations should be taken while setting up a new school.

Sports facilities for general public should not be more than walking distance from their residential areas. They should be able to reach it say within 20 or 25 minutes.

Sports facilities are also provided on a large scale for a large number of people or for a town or city at one central place. Here, training is imparted, competitions are held and the sports facilities are utilized by people who are seriously interested in sports. The place is visited by spectators. At the time of planning such playgrounds, due consideration should be paid to the approach roads.

GEOGRAPHICAL FACTORS

Geographical factors are of great importance in deciding the location of a play ground. The location of an industry nearby, blowing of wind, position of sun etc. have to be given due consideration.

The playing field should be located at such a place so that smoke or exhaust gases do not pollute the healthy atmosphere of the playing field. Direction and speed of the wind should be taken into account while reaching a decision.

If the wind blows hard, it will interfere with sports. So this should also be given due consideration.

Fields have to be irrigated. It is advantageous if water is closeby. To prevent balls from falling into water, nets or trees can be erected.

Some areas are infested with worms insects, gnats etc. The land can be eliminated of these creatures by use of insects, pests chemicals. But the remedy is only for a short time. The land will again revert to its earlier position. So it is not advisable to making playing fields on such ground.

The direction of the sun is also an important factor to be noted while planning a playing field. It should not be in such a position that its rays produce a glare in the eyes of the players in the morning, afternoon and evening because these are the times when games are played. In track and field events, it is particularly necessary to know the direction and intensity of the wind. These are laid down for competition in such fields. If this requirement is not met, competition cannot be held. If necessary, planting of trees can also be resorted to meet the problem to some extent. The sun goes from east to west, so the ground should be in the north-south axis.

It is essential that all these factors are taken into account otherwise it will not be possible to make full/proper use of the facility.

NATURE OF THE SOIL ON THE SITE

It is also very important to examine the nature of the soil before selecting the location of a playing field. It should fulfill the following requirements.

(i) satisfactory thickness of the top soil of the ground.
(ii) easy excavation of the earth.
(iii) Permeability of the earth so that water is soaked quickly.
(iv) water level below the surface of the earth. It should be at least 70 cm.
(v) as far as possible, the ground should be plain. A sloppy ground involves a large amount of work to set it right.

It is advisable not to waste aerable land for such purposes when waste land or land of inferior quality can serve the purpose. The best soil for play ground is grassy. Loamy sand soils with thick layer of top soil are best suited. The soil should not be of pat variety as the turf remains loose and does not form a dense velvet lawn. Further, it feels spongy on walking and is likely to break open from the ground.

REMARKS ON DESIGN AND CONSTRUCTION

Sports are not merely for the improvement of physical health. Many a qualities are associated with it. It develops the mind and inculcates many worth - while characteristics. So it is much associated with culture. With this in view, a playing ground should be located in a beautiful area.

Greenery and trees are the first factor which should be looked for. It will look beautiful to the mind and give it calmness and joy. It will be healthy for the eyes. It will also purify the atmosphere. It is better still if there is some lake around or some natural beauty. The area around should preferably not be congested.

In construction a playing field, the structure of the buildings around should not be over - looked. The construction of the playing field should not be in contrast with but should be in harmony with its environment and should add to its charm and beauty. This is a job for an architect who is well-versed in such type of activity.

If all the factors are taken into consideration,the playing field and the area around will add to the beauty and charm of the town or city.

DIMENSIONS OF SPORTS FACILITIES

We can think of a large scale stadium which caters for all types of sports or of some small scale playing fields. This is centralization and de-centralization of sport facilities. Both these extremes are not advisable.

Some towns and cities have much population. The roads are congested and if the sport facilities are centralized, much distance will have to be covered. This will all add to the inconvenience of the sports lovers. This will, however, not be the case if many sports facilities are provided at different places. People can easily reach the play ground.

The construction of a large number of playing fields have also its disadvantages. The greatest factor is economic as most of the facilities provided in a centralized play ground will have to be provided for the de-centralized playing grounds. Extra expenses will have to be incurred on the care and maintenance of the playing fields. A large number of sports field keepers will have to be employed. Large number of equipment will also have to be required. The total area of land required for providing sports facilities would be much greater.

The best course is the mid way to provide a central sports facility as well as reasonable number of playing fields at appropriate distances.

Many types of sports facilities are provided. Some require greater area whereas others require small areas. The area required for a sport ground has to take into consideration the sports for which the facilities are to be provided. Riding, motoring, cycling and golf require much areas. Combined facilities can be provided for a number of games as track, field athletics and playing. This is recommend for school, mass sports and competition. Then special fields have to be provided for different games as cricket, hockey, foot-ball, volley ball, basket ball, tennis, badminton and other small field games. Playing field should also include fields for exercise. Separate fields for competition should be segregated from that which caters for training. This will prevent the former from undue use.

MATERIAL FOR THE CONSTRUCTION OF SPORTS FACILITIES

A large variety of material is required for construction purpose. One must be aware of all these materials and where they are available at cheap rates. As transportation adds much to the cost of material, it is necessary to find out where it can be available at a nearby place. These are important factors as these add to the cost of construction.

It is necessary to know the composition and application of these materials. These are indicated in the table below :

Materials	*Composition, Properties*	*Applications*
Sands (Ø 0.1 to 3.0 mm)		
River sand	Containing quartz and humus particles	Soft pits, esp. pits for shot-put
Foundry sand	Quartz sand with cohesive components (clayey)	Soft pits
Wind-blown sand	Almost pure quartz sand. No cementing properties, hard, angular	Addition to soft pits. Surface of hard courts and running tracks
Tuff sand	Cementing, soft, non-elastic	Barn-floor type surfacing, surfacing layer, and running tracks
Quicksand, shifting sand	Micaceous, containing water	Shot-put pits
Crused stone sand	Smallest particles of crushed rock, angular, hard	Hard courts
Gravel (Ø 4 to 70 mm)		
Fine gravel, coarse gravel	Varies largely, de-pending on local conditions	Middle layer of hard courts and running tracks. Haunching of drainage pipes. Fabrication of concrete
Stone chips (Ø up to 30 mm)	Angular, normally poor in water retention	Middle layer of hard courts and running

Materials	*Composition, Properties*	*Applications*
		tracks. Haunching of drainage pipes. Fabrication of concrete.
Earth Clay	Alumina, siliceous earth and water. Impervious, watercontaining, cementing	Binder component of all surfacings
Loam	Clay, sand (can be felt), humus, and water. Impervious, cementing	Binder component of all surfacings
Marl	Clay, limestone (calcium carbonate), and sand. Cementing,impervious, non-elastic, hard	Surfacing layers and binder agent for soft pits
Humus	Organic and mineral components, water-retaining, pass on water only slowly, rich in bacteria, cementing	Binder component of all surfacings. (Not more than 20% of the whole mass)
Peat	Primarily organic component. Limeless acid, water-containing; fails to pass on water, cementing	Improvement of light soils
Cinders		
Locomotive ashes	Fine-gained, cementing, low density	Filling agent for surfacing layers
Filter ashes	Fine-grained, permeable to water	Filling material for surfacing layers
Furnace clinker, boilerhouse cinders	Permeable to water and water-containing. Coarse or fine particles, depending on degree of reduction	Lower and middle layers of surfacings of running tracks and hard courts

Materials	*Composition, Properties*	*Applications*
Blast-furnace slag	High density, permeable to water, black or red colour	In ground condition used as filling material for running track surfacing
Other Materials		
Crushed clay brick, brick dust	Burned loam or clay products water-absorbing, coloured	Ideal material for middle layer of surfacing, filling material for running track and hard court surfacings
Clay containing silt	Organic and mineral constituents, water-absorbing, cementing	Cementing agent for all surfacings
Bitumen	Acid-resisting, practically non water-absorbing, cementing, deep black	Playgrounds; surfacings of playing fields, running tracks, paths and roads
Asphalt	Acid-resisting, practically non water-absorbing, cementing, deep black	

CHAPTER-4

PLANS AND DESCRIPTIONS OF PLAYING FIELDS

ARCHERY

Archery is a game of ancient times. The competitor enjoys target hunting as well as become an expert in hunting.

Three lanes are drawn and these are at least 5m. in width. These are about 100m. long. At one end is the waiting line and the permanent shorting line is at least 5m. distance from it. Five lines are drawn across the lanes at a distance of 30m, 50m, 60m, 70m and 90m from the permanent shooting line. Two shooting targets are placed in one lane at 90m. line.

The shooting area for men and women is separated by at least 10m. lane. The distance from shooting line for women is 70m, 60m, 50m and 30m.

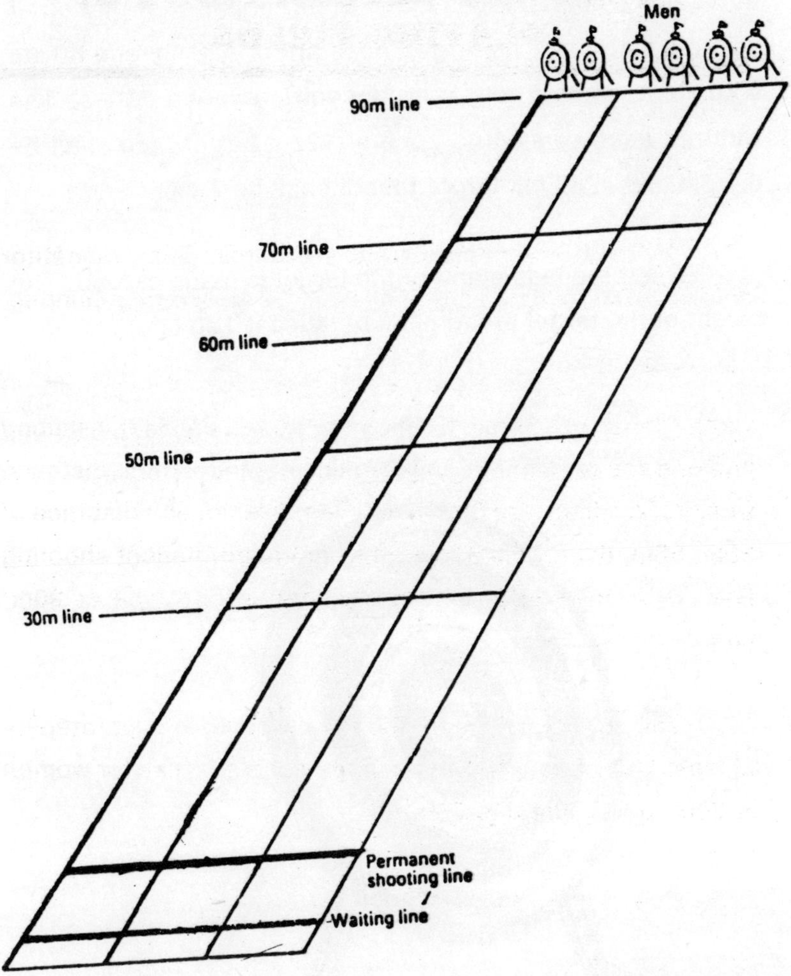
Men
90m line
70m line
60m line
50m line
30m line
Permanent shooting line
Waiting line

The target comprises of straw ropes stitched together. It has five coloured faces made either of paper or any other suitable material. The target faces are of 122 cm and 80 cm diameters, divided into ten concentric scoring zones. The width of each concentric zone in 122m target face shall be 6.1 cm and in 80 cm target face it shall be 4 cm.

The three legs stand of the target is made of food. The height of the target stand shall be atleast 130 cm

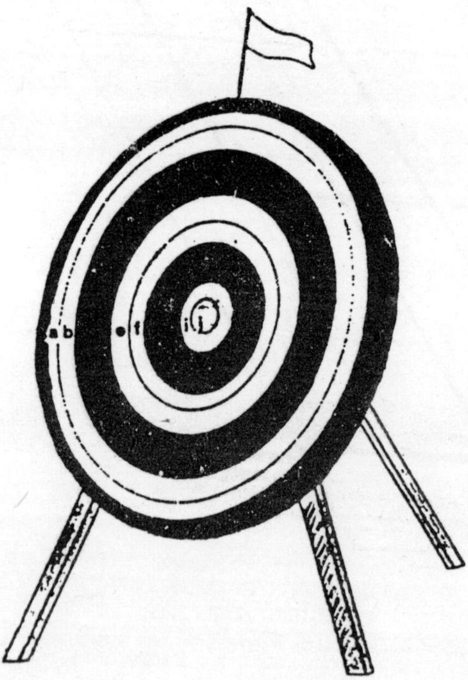

The points awarded for concentrated circle are as under : -

a	White (Outer)	1 Point
b	White (Inner)	2 Points
c	Black (Outer)	3 Points
d	Blue (Outer)	5 Points
f	Blue (Inner)	6 Points
g	Red (Outer)	7 Points
h	Red (Inner)	8 Points
i	Gold (Outer)	9 Points
j	Gold (Inner)	10 Points

The figure of the 122 cm target face is give below.

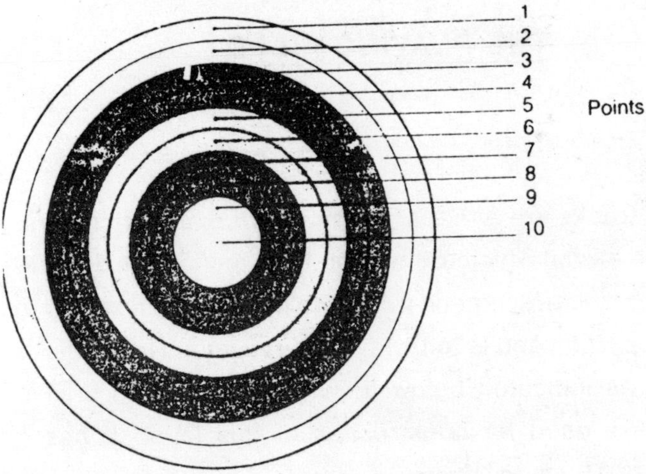

122cm. Target Face

■■■■■■■■■■■

CHAPTER-5

ATHLETICS

In athletics are included large number of events. These events can be classified in two categories - track and field. Track events are those which are played on the track inside the stadium. These include races - sprint races, middle distance races, long distance races and relays and hurdles. The field event are those which are played either inside or outside area of the track or outside the stadium. Events such as jumping, throwing, walks and road races come within this category.

THE PLAYING FIELD

TRACKS

The tracks are either of grass or are made of cinders/ synthetic material which are not too hard and are skid proof. For making cinder/synthetic track, the material is mixed up in proper proportion and is to be laid in three layers of requisite thickness as indicated below. Lower Layer broken bricks/ concrete are used for construction of this layer. It has a thickness of 15 cm to 20 cm.

Intermediate Layer. Crushed clay bricks are used for laying this layer. This layer is about 15 cm.

Top layer. This layer is between 6 cm to 10 cm and is made up of the aggregate and the binder soil. The aggregate consists of half burnt coal cinder, red bajri, crushed bricks and brick dust. The binder soil is of powdered clay. The aggregate and clay should be mixed in the ration of 3:1.

The material used can vary and the thickness of the layers depends on the nature of the material. Whenever 8 lane track is laid, a 4 lane track should also be laid for training. All competitions of international importance are now-a-days held on synthetic tracks.

The main track of 8 lanes is of 400 m in circumference. It is used both for competition and training. The other 4 lane track which is exclusively meant for training is 200 m in circumference.

The length and breadth of the main track are 175.40 m x 96.40 m. Two semi-circles of radius 38.20 m are drawn at two ends and these are joined by two straight lines, each 79 m long.

The width of each lane is 1.22 m to 1.25 m. The width of 8 lanes, therefore, works out to 9.76 m to 10.00 m.

A border is made on the inside of the first lane of the track. It is made of cement and metal and should be 5 cm. in height as well as in width. The track should have a slope - 1:100 laterally and 1:1000m in either direction.

The inside and outside areas of the track are used for jumping and throwing events. For all the races which are run around, the start is staggered. The competitors are expected to run in their lanes. If they touch their line or cross it, they will be disqualified. The races are run in anticlock-wise direction and come to an end at a fixed point.

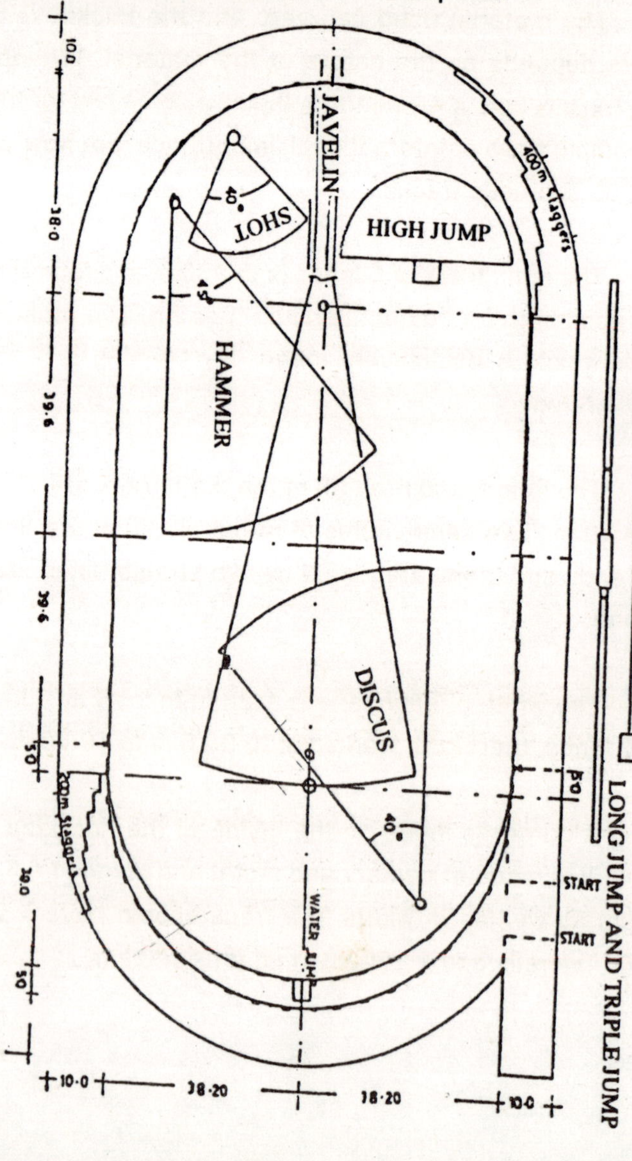

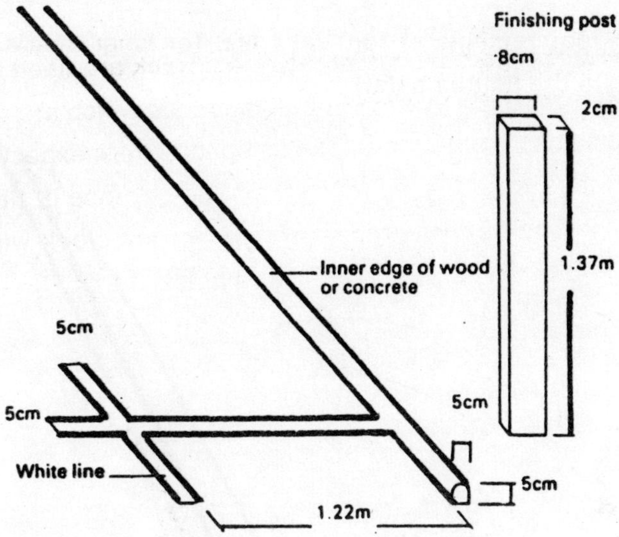

LONG AND TRIPLE JUMP

The length and width of the runway should be 45mx1.22m. It should be marked by white lines of width 50 mm. The runway is made of the same material as that used in the construction of track.

The take off is 20 cm in width and is made of wood. The edge of the board nearest to the pit is called the take-off line. Then comes the plasticine indicator. This portion has a width of 10 cm. It has a tray which is fitted with plasticine or some soft substance. If the player does not jump from the take-off board and his foot crosses the take-off line, his fault is recorded on plasticine of the material. Next is left a portion of 70 cm before the landing pit starts. The length of the landing pit is 9 m. It is about 2.75 m wide. It is fitted with fine clean sand.

The requirements of run ways etc. for long jump are illustrated in the figures below :-

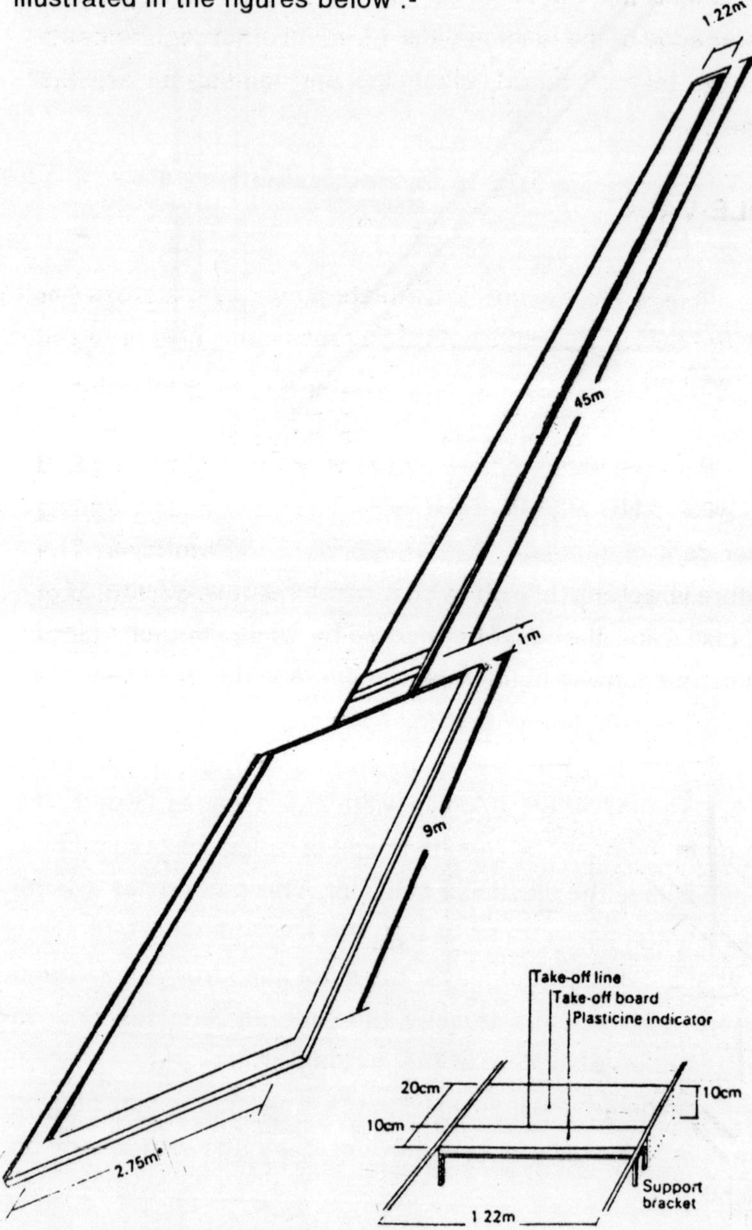

In the case of triple jump, the only difference from the long jump is that the distance from the take-off board and the nearer edge of the landing pit is 13 m. All other requirements such as take-off board, plasticine and landing pit are the same.

POLE VAULT

In pole vault event, the athlete jumps over a cross bar with the help of a flexible pole. The cross bar is held between the two uprights. The cross bar is raised after each jump.

For pole vaulting, the runway is at least 45 m long and 2 m wide. The last 5 m of the runway is stabilized by adding 5 per cent of cements to the material of the top layer. The mixture is well wetted, spread over the area, compacted, kept wet until it is set and is rolled frequently. The pole vault facility is illustrated in the figure below.

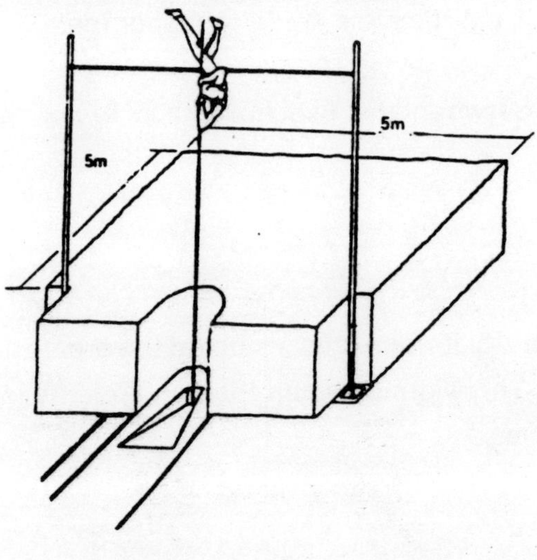

The wooden box for planting the hole between the runway and the landing pit.

The dimensions of the box are : -

Length	100 cm
Width of the approach raod	60 cm
Width of the pit side	15 cm
Depth at the pit side	20 cm

Board and end-board are at right angle.

To allow the water to drain from the box, two holes are arranged at the bottom. When the box is not in use, it is covered to protect it from rain.

The landing pit is square in size with minimum length of 5 cm. Its height is 1 m. The pit is made of rubber foam.

The distance between the two upright is between 3.66 m-4.04 m.

HIGH JUMP

In high jump the athlete who crosses bar at the greatest height is the winner. The width between the two uprights is between 3.66 m-4.04m.

The runway is made of the same materials as that of the track. The materials are also mixed in the same proportion.

A circular approach run is arranged as shown in the figure below.

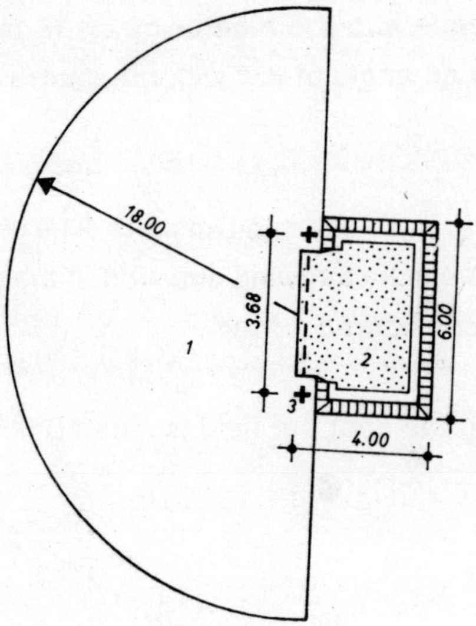

High-jump facility

1 Runway 2 Pit 3 Jumping stand

The athlete is to run a distance of 18 m before he takes a jump from the centre of the pit. The take-off place is exposed to high stress. So cement about 5 per cent in quantity is added to the material to stabilize its position. The cement is set in the same way as in the case of pole vault.

The landing pit is made of rubber foam and is 6 m in length, 4 m in width and 70 cm in height.

SHOT PUT

The shot should be put from a circle and land within the marked sector. The circle has a diameter of 2.135 m. The throwing sector makes an angle of 65° with the centre of the throwing circle.

The throwing circle is divided into two parts. The dividing line is at right angle to the main throwing direction. If the player crosses this line, it is considered a fault.

A sketch showing the shot put field is given below.

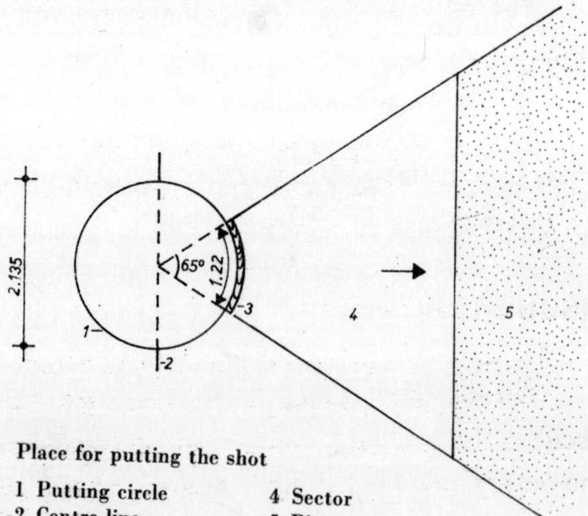

Place for putting the shot

1 Putting circle
2 Centre line
3 Putting beam
4 Sector
5 Pit

In the front of the circle touching the inner edge of the throwing board is a wooden board. It limits the circle. The throwing board has spikes which are driven into the ground. Boards are put into sleeves which are inserted into the ground. The height of the board is 10.2 cm and its width is 11.4 cm. The inner edge when stretched is 1.22 m long. The board is white painted.

To prevent the shot from sinking deeply in the pit within the throwing sector, the pit should be filled with alluvial sand, foundry sand, loamy sand or river sand having fine grain size. The top layer should be hardened so that the shot leaves only a small depression. This is done by the addition of cement.

The pit should be provided with wooden or concrete borders.

To enable easy measurement of the distance of throw of the shot, the throwing sector is divided with lines marked at a distance of 1 m from each other.

DISCUS THROWING

For discus throwing, there is a circle from which the discus is thrown and ground on which the discus is thrown. The outer portion of the circle is made of iron steel or some other suitable material. The inner portion of the circle is made of concrete of any other non-slippery material. The diameter of the circle is 2.50 cm. As in the case of shot put, the circle is bisected by a line and if the player crosses this line while throwing the discus, the throw will become invalid. Similarly, the throwing sector forms an angle of 60° at the centre of the circle and is marked by lines to facilitate measurement of the distance of throw. The lines of the marked sector should be 5 cm wide.

The throwing sector should be flat and in level. A protective cage can also be provided if the discus is likely to hit anyone. A sketch of the discus throwing place is given below.

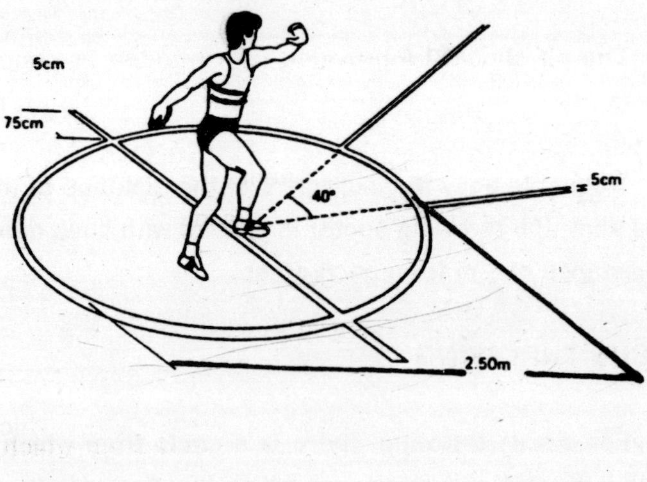

HAMMER THROWING

The circle for throwing the hammer is of the same dimension as that of shot put. The throwing sector also forms the same angle at the centre of the circle. The only difference from the shot put is that it is not provided with a wooden stop board.

The head of the hammer is made of steel and is attached to a steel wire. The hammer circle is provided with a cage made of metal strips mounted on metal supports of minimum 3.35 m in height as indicated in the figure below.

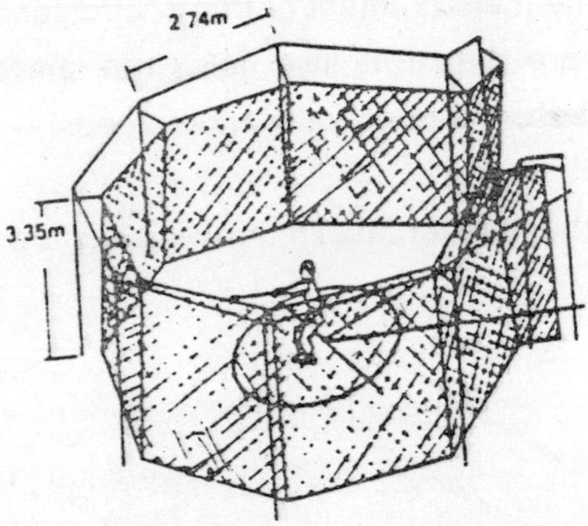

The metal strips should be strong to afford high power resistance to absorb the force of throw.

JAVELIN THROWING

The field for javeling throwing has runway and an area of throwing the javeline. The runway is at least 30 m in length and 4 m in width. At the end of the run way, there is the board of throw which is made of metal or wood and is painted white. It has a width of 7 cm and is in the form of an arc having a radius of 8 m. It is provided with steel spikes to fix it in the ground. The sector for throwing has an angle of 28° from the centre of the arc. From the outer end of the arc 1.50 m long and 7 cm wide lines are drawn at right angle to the direction of the runway.

To help in the measurement of throw, circular arcs at a distance of 5 m are drawn. It also helps the spectators to guess the result before it is actually announced.

A figure of the field for javelin throwing is shown below.

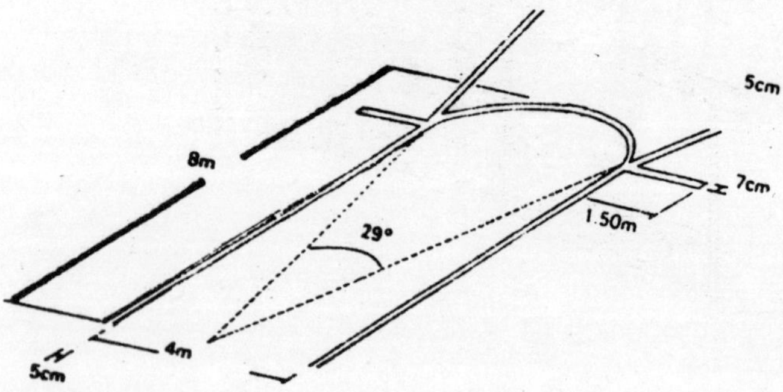

HURDLES

The hurdles are of steel with its top made of wood. The wooden top is 1.20 m long and 7 cm wide. The wooden bar is stripped in black and white. The height of the hurdle is adjustable. It is adjusted according to the length of the race and sex of the player. There are two hurdle events - For men there are 110 m and 400 m and for women these are 100 m and 400 m. In men's hurdle for 110 m, the height of the hurdles is 106.7 cm and they are kept 9.14 m apart. In women's hurdle for 100 m, the height of the hurdles is 84 cm and they are kept 8.5 m apart. In 400 hurdle event, the height of the hurdles is 91.4 cm for men and for women the height is 76.2 cm. In both the cases, the hurdles are kept 35 m apart.

A sketch of the hurdle is given in the figure below.

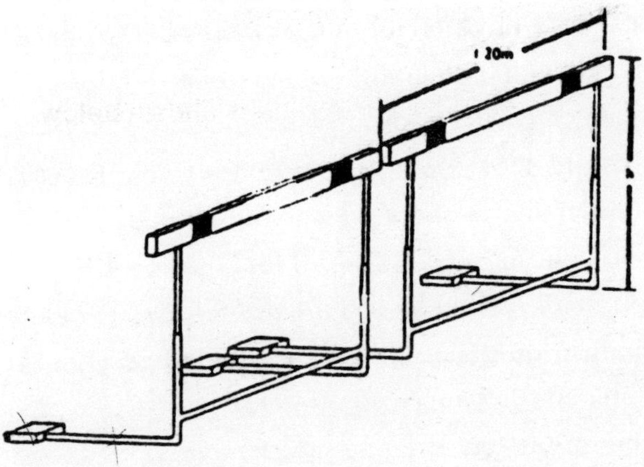

STEEPLE CHASE

The steeple chase hurdle is made of wood. The base of the hurdle on either side is about 1.40 m. The top bar is 3.66 m long and about 13 cm wide. The hurdle has a height of 91.4 cm. The maximum weight of the hurdle should be 100 kg. A sketch of the hurdle is given below.

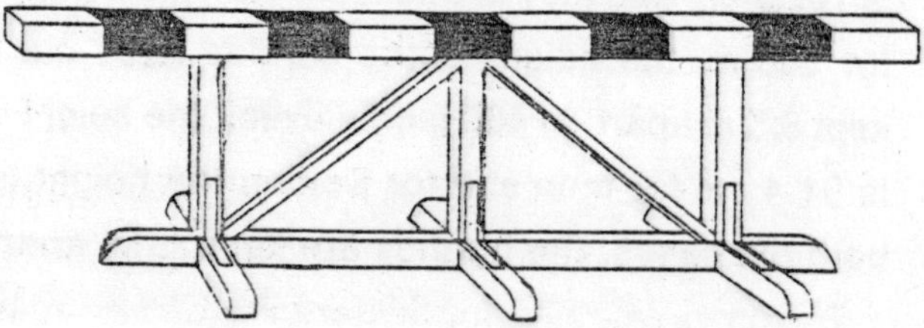

The competitors have to run a distance of 3000 m. it involves 28 jumps over hurdles and 7 jumps over a ditch.

The ditches are provided adjacent to the track. So the course for steeple chase is changed a little.

The distance from the start to the first round should not have any obstacle. The course of track changes in accordance with the number of obstacles. The water jump is arranged in the curve at a distance from the finish.

The five obstacles are at a distance of 84 m from one another. The distance from the start to the beginning of the first round is 60 m. Accordingly, the distance of 3000 m is worked out as under.

length of one round	=	420 m
length of 7 rounds	=	2,940 m
Distance from start to the beginning of the first round.	=	60 m
		3,000 m

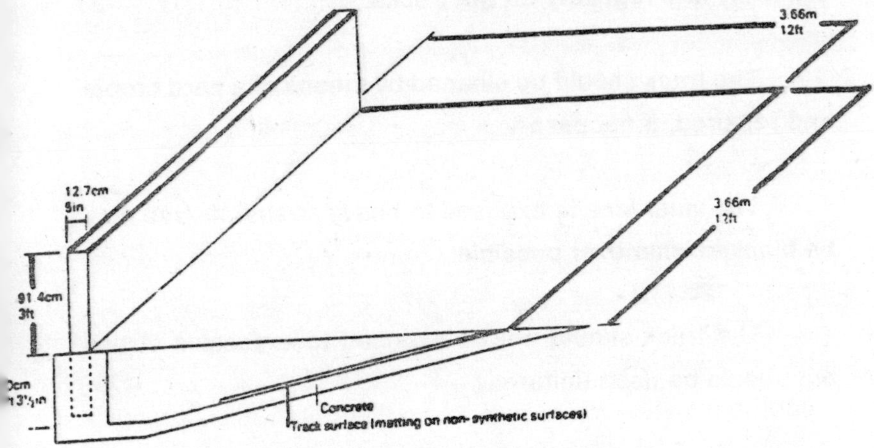

The landing place is 1.50 m within the pit and .50 m on the running track. The water jump has a coconut mat so that feet are not injured. The top layer is that of concrete and the lower one is made of gravel. It has a connection to drainage system.

MAINTENANCE OF RUNNING TRACKS, PITS AND AREAS FOR THROWING

It is necessary to maintain carefully the running tracts, pits and areas for throwing. If considered necessary, a sport-field keeper may be appointed. If this is done, expensive repairs can be avoided.

Weeds are uprooted by means of implements and if necessary by use of chemicals.

During the hot season, water should be sprinkled uniformly and regularly on the tracks.

The track should be cleaned by means of a hard broom and repaired, if necessary.

The inner lane is exposed to heavy stress. Its use may be blocked whenever possible.

The track should not be exposed to excessive stress but should be used uniformly.

Sports person use the same spot again and again as in throwing events. This should be avoided and all facilities should be utilised uniformly.

Special attention has to be paid to the tracks during the rainy season. After the rain, the track is levelled and pieces of stone and slag are removed. Top course material is added to the surface, if considered necessary The track should be rolled by means of a light roller. If the rain is heavy and drainage of water becomes difficult, holes are dug for providing additional drainage.

Large number of implements such as lawn mower,hand roller, heavy roller, spiked roller, lawn sprinklers are required for care and maintenance for track and field athletics.

For care and maintenance of running track and hard fields, additional implements such as towed nets mats and broom, spiked board, u-iron for skimming and rotary hoe are required. A small tractor for carrying implements and material might be necessary.

CHAPTER-6

BADMINTON

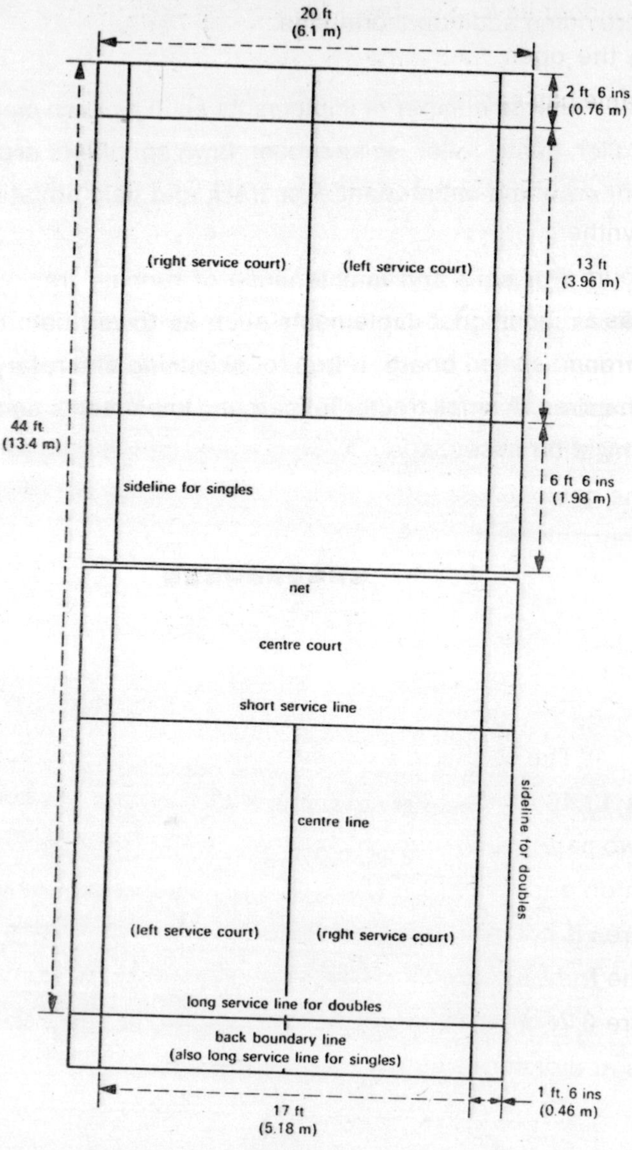

Badminton is a game which is played with a racket and a shuttlecock. As the shuttlecock is light, the game can be easily disturbed by wind. So, all competitive games are held in indoor halls. For training purposes matches can be played in the open. As it requires a small area, provision for this game can easily be made along with other games in the open.

The indoor halls have a floor of wooden planks or synthetic courts of approved specifications and material. The court should be above the floor to the extent of say 9m. It has a number of windows to admit natural light. Proper lighting arrangement is also made. It should not produce glare or cast shadows as to interfere in the concentration of the players. Any wind from the windows or otherwise should not disturb the game. A space of at least 2 m should be left between the boundary wall and the base line.

The dimensions of the badminton court are shown in figure of last page.

The court can be used both for singles and doubles. It is 13.40 m long and 6.10 m wide. The court is divided into two parts, each side being 6.70 m long. The side line of 0.46 m on each side of the width is for doubles. For singles, this area is not included. The rear service line is for singles while the front service line is for doubles. These two service lines are 0.76 m apart. The front service line or short service line is at a distance of 1.98 m from the net.

The area between the short service line and the rear service line for singles is equally divided. These are the left and right service courts.

The ground should be marked in yellow or white and the width of the lines should be 40 mm.

The net is 6.10 m long and 76 cm wide. It is made of cord of 1.9 cm mesh. It is fixed on the centre line. The upper edge of the net (at post) is 1.55 m and the minimum distance of the net at its centre is 1.52 m from the ground. The two posts holding the net are fixed outside the boundary line of the court. The posts are made of suitable material so that they can hold the net in its stretched position.

■■■■■■■■■■■

CHAPTER-7

BASEBALL

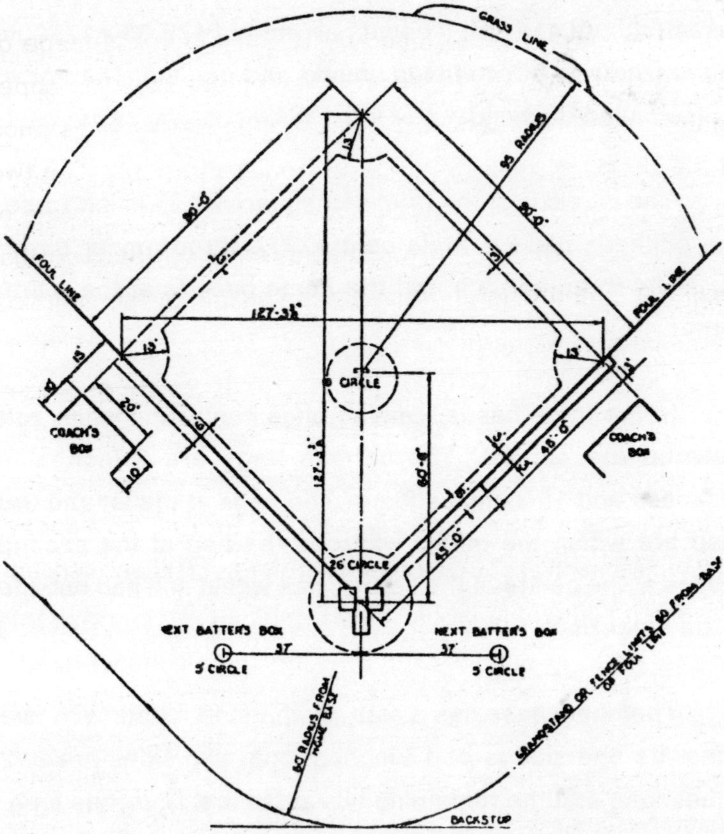

The game is normally not played in Indian or any other part of the world except in U.S.A. and Japan. It is the official national sport of the former. It is a bat and ball game and is played by two teams of nine members.

A baseball field includes player's box, batter's box, pitcher's plate, home base, player's line and three runner bases-Ist, 2nd and 3rd. It covers an area of 175.00 x 12500m and is made up of two fields, infield and outfield. The infield is also called diamond.

The infield is of the form of a square 27.25 m long side. The pitcher's plate is in its centre. The three runner bases are at its three corners and the home base is at the fourth corner.

In the three bases, canvas bags containing white soft material are placed. The canvas bags are 5 inches in thickness and 15 inches square. The bags at the Ist and 3rd base are within the infield whereas the bag at the second base is at the centre of the corner, half within and half outside of the inner field.

The home base has a slab of whitened rubber with five sides. Its one side is of 17 inches long, two sides are $8^1/2$ inches long and the remaining two sides are 12 inches long. The home base plate is placed such that its 17 inch edge faces the pitcher plate. Its 12 inches edge coincides with the Ist and 3rd bases. The distance between home base to 2nd base and the Ist to 3rd base is 127 ft. 3-3/8 inches. The pitcher plate which is 10 inches above the degree of its slope should be one inch to one foot towards the home plate.

The out field is formed by extending the foul lines at the Ist and 3rd corner of the infield. The distance between the home base to centre field fence is 400 feet or more, and 320 feet or more along the foul line.

The battery's box is situated partly within the infield and partly in the outfield at the home base corner. The catcher box is also in the outfield below the home base.

CHAPTER-8

BASKETBALL

FULL SIZE REGULATION COURT

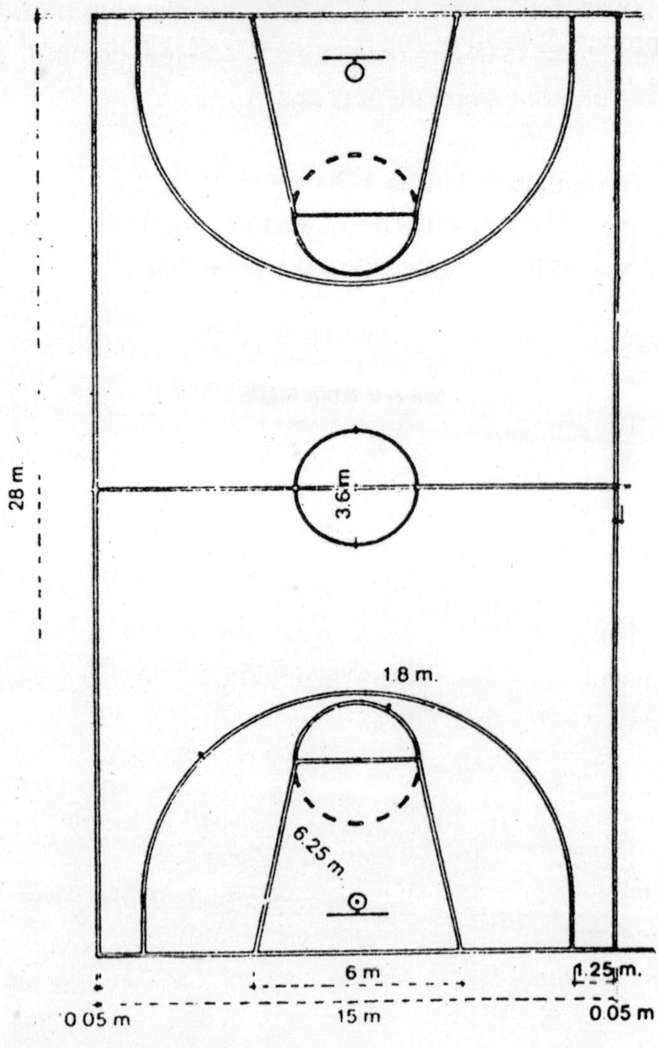

Grass field is not used for playing basket ball because grass hinders fast play and also there is danger of players being slipped. It is a hard field when the game is played in the open. The surface can be made of concrete, asphalt or earth. The game is also played indoor. In that case the floor is wooden. The height of the ceiling should be atleast 7m and proper ventilation and lighting arrangements should be made.

The court is 26 mm in length and 147 mm in width. A space of 2.00 m. is added to the outer lines. A centre line divides the court in two equal parts. There are two circles at the middle of the centre line. The inner and outer circles have a radius of .60 m and 1.80 m respectively.

The free throw line has a width of 6 m at the base line and 3.60 m at the free throw line. The distance between the base line and the free throw line is 5.80 m. The latter forms the diameter of the circumscribed circle.

The uprights alongwith backboard and ring should be at a distance of 1 m from the outer edge of the end lines and 1.20 m from the base line into the court. As these should be clearly visible to the players, these should be of bright colour.

The board is made either of wood or plastic. It is 1.20 m. in length. 1.80 m in width and 3 cm in thickness. The surface is smooth and of white colour. A basket is fastened to the backboard at a height 3.05 m from the ground. A rectangle 0.59 m horizontally and 0.45 m vertically is drawn above the opening of the basket to keep in throwing the ball in the basket.

The basket consists of a white cord net. The ring from which it is suspended is made of iron and has inner diameter of 45 cm.

The supports are mainly made of steel tubes or aluminium. Supports made of wood or concrete can also be provided.

The width of the lines should be at least 5 cms and these should be clearly visible.

CHAPTER-9

BOXING

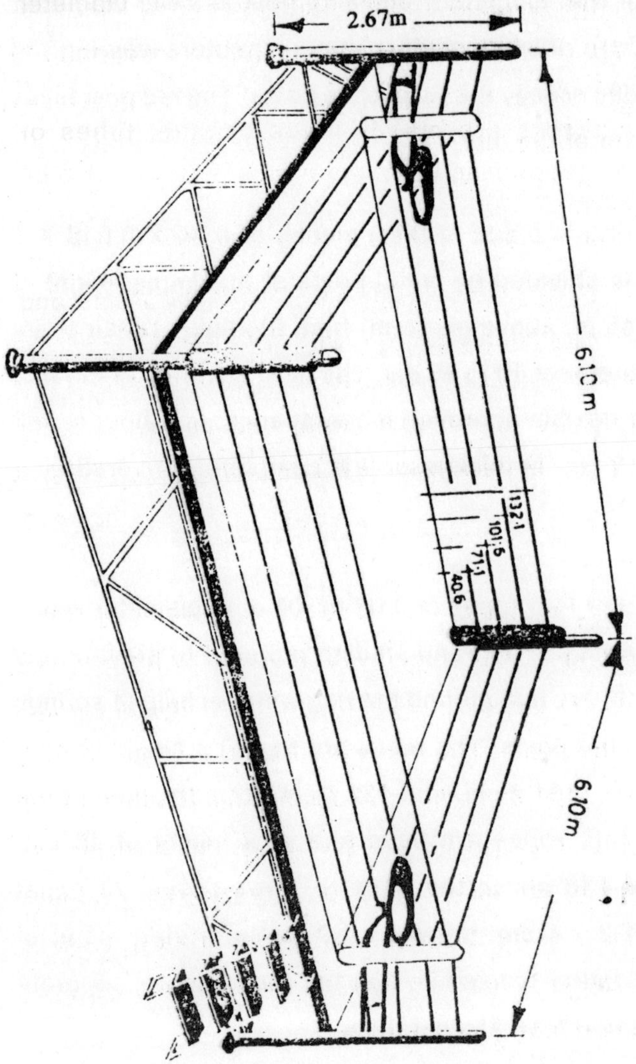

The game is played in a boxing ring. It is of two types, platform and floor. The platform is at a height between 91 to 1.22 m. It is a rectangular ring of size between 5 m to 6 m. It has posts at four corners. The colour of a corner post is red and that of the diagonally opposite post is blue. The other two posts are of white colour. The competitors wearing red and blue belts occupy the respective posts. The red post faces the president of the jury.

The ring is made of thick planks of 0.30 X 0.038 X 7 meters. It is shielded by metal posts of maximum height of 2.67 m (1.45 m. above platform) from the floor. These posts have a diameter of 10 to 15 cm. The floor covering of the ring consists of flexible approved material such as rubber or felt of 1.3 to 1.9 cm. in thickness. It is completely covered by a canvas.

Three or four ropes of 0.03 to .05 m in diameter which have a covering of soft and smooth material to prevent any rope scratch, are tied around the ring with the help of springs attached to the posts. The ropes are tied at a height of 40.6 cm., 71.1 cm., 101.6 cm. and 132.1 cm. from the floor of the ring when four ropes are used and at a height of 40 cm, 80 cm and 130 cm in the case of three ropes. At equal distance of 3 - 4 cm. between the ropes, a strip made of canvas or leather is fixed so that the ropes do not separate when the boxer lean against them.

Stool is provided at the red and blue corners for the competitors. Two ladders are also provided for their use. A ladder is provided at a white corner for use of referees and doctors.

CHAPTER-10

CRICKET

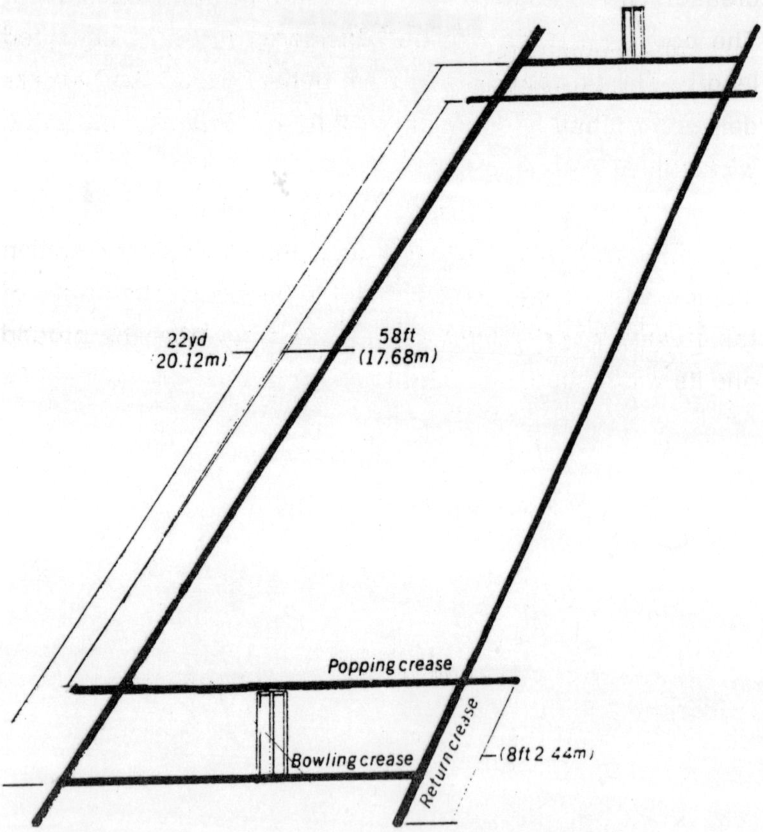

A cricket field can be of any size ranging from 80.00 to 150.00 m in length and 60.00 to 100.00 m in breadth. The two wickets are arranged in the middle at a distance of 20.12 m from each other. The ground between the wickets called pitch is normally of a lawn type grass. The width of the pitch is approximately 3.30 m. At either end of the pitch is a popping crease. It is rectangular and is 2.64 m wide and 1.22 m deep. The popping crease can be considered to be of unlimited length. The bowling crease from behind which the bowlers delivers the ball has a width of 2.02 m. Its limitation is the wicket line.

The wickets consists of a set of three cylindrical wooden stumps with two bails at each end of the pitch. The height of the stumps when fixed should be 71.1 cm from the ground and its width should be 22.86 cm.

CHAPTER-11

FENCING

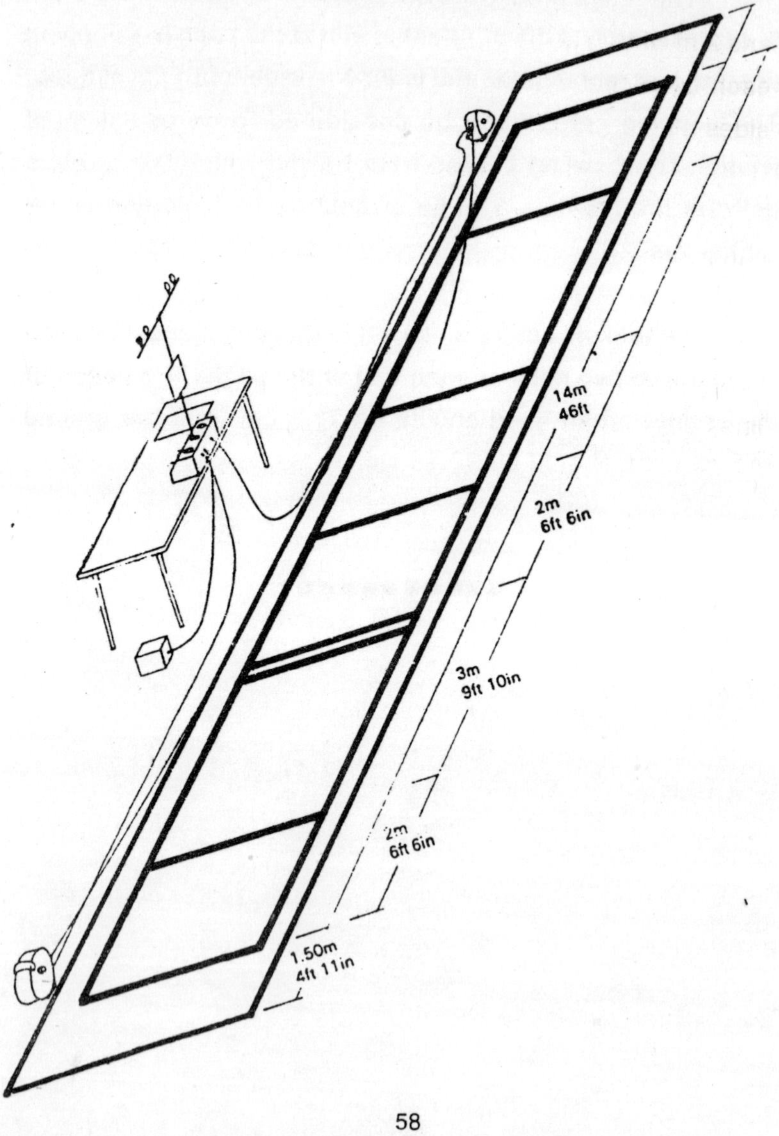

The game involves attack by sword and defence and is played throughout the world. It is included in the olympic games.

The playing field which is called " Piste " is 14 m long and 2 m wide. The field is divided in two halves in length of 7 m each by a central line. From the central line, lines on both sides are drawn at a distance of 2 m,3 m and 2 m.

The surface of the field should be smooth and flat. It can be made of rubber, plastic, metallic mesh, linoleum and wood. The field can be either outdoor or indoor.

At the beginning of the match, the players stand at the lines 2 m away from the central line.

CHAPTER-12

FOOTBALL

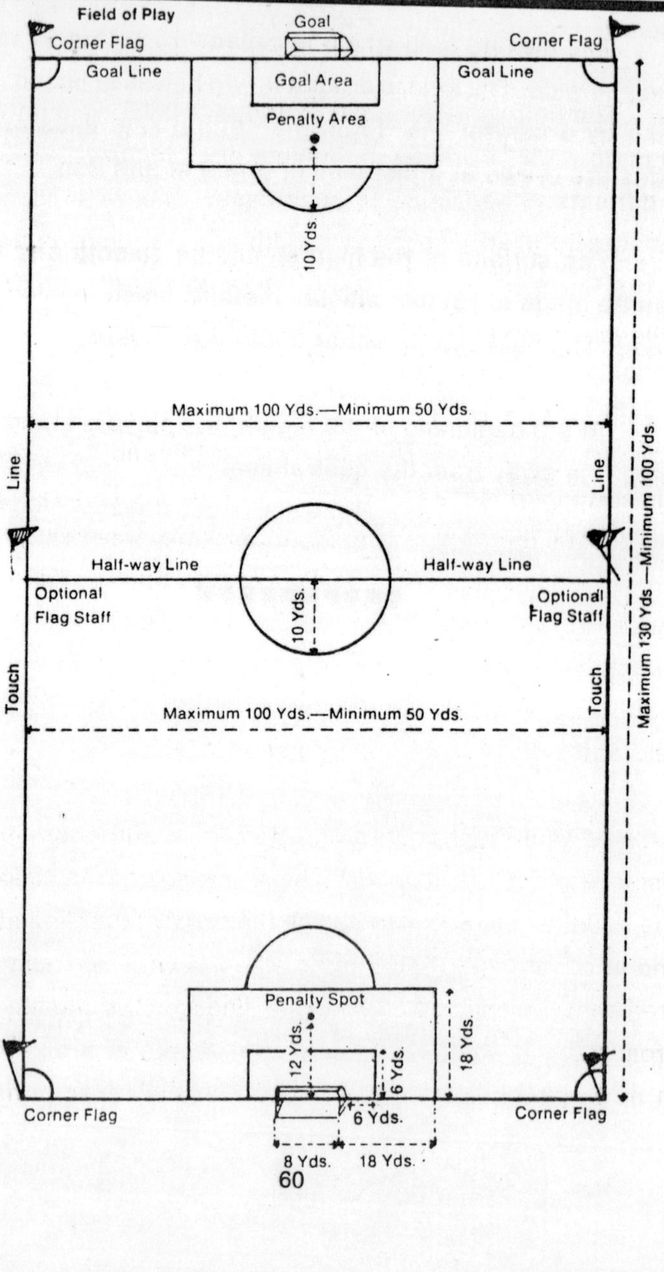

Grassfields as well as hard fields are used for playing football. Grass fields are, however, preferred. Hard fields are mainly used for training. This is necessary for the growth of grass.

The field is rectangular in shape, 105 m. in length and 70 m. in width. For women, juniors and children, the field is of different dimensions. In such cases, the dimensions are not standardized. Length and width are, however, to be kept in the ratio of 3 : 2. The other areas and goals have dimensions proportional to the dimensions of the complete fields.

The complete field is 105 m in length and 75 m in width. It is surrounded by a 2 m wide strip. A centre line or half way line divides the field in two equal parts. A circle with 9.15 m radius is marked in the middle of the centre line. This is called kick off circle. The corners of the field are marked by a quarter circle of radius 1 m. Four flag posts at the four corners of the field and two flag posts at a distance of 1 m off the field at the ends of the centre line are fixed.

At each goal post, a line parallel to the goal line at a distance of 5.50 m is drawn. The rectangular area inside this line and the goal line is called goal area. Another line at each end at a distance of 16.5 m. is also drawn. The rectangular area between this line and the goal line is called penalty area. From the mid point of the goal line, a spot at a distance of 11 m is marked in the penalty area. This is called penalty mark. An arc of a circle with penalty mark as centre and a radius of 9.15 m is drawn outside the penalty area.

The half way line, the kick of circle, the goal area and penalty areas must be visibly marked. The borders of the field should be clearly visible lines about 12 cm wide.

The internal dimensions of the goal are as under.

Height up to the lower edge of the cross bar - 2.44 cm
Distance between the posts - 7.32 cm

The two goal posts and the cross bar must have a thickness of 12.5 m and is made of wood. Round timber is not allowed. It should be white in colour,

The nets are attached to the posts. These are made of hemp, jute or nylon.

■■■■■■■■■■■

CHAPTER-13

GOLF

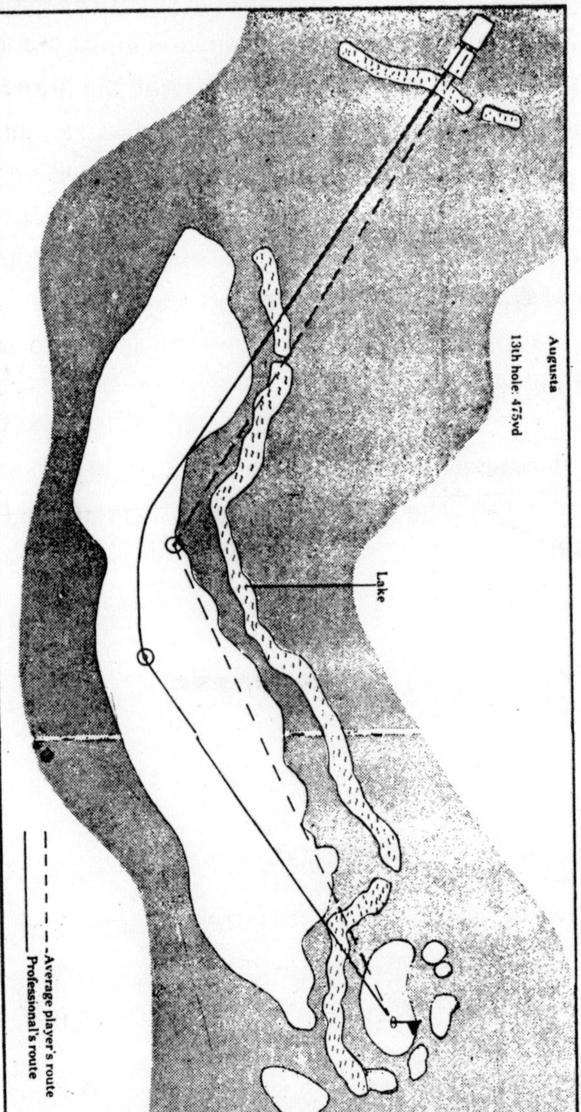

Golf is a game involving a stick and a ball. It can be played either individually or in a team of 2 to 4 players.

The golf field has not a definite shape. The area may vary according to the local conditions and the area available. The boundary should be clearly defined. It should have 18 holes. The distance between the holes should be between 100 - 600 yd. The field comprises different areas of different nature. At the rectangular area, the play begins. It is followed by other types of areas, fair rough and hazards - bunkers, trees, water, etc. and green alongwith hole into which the player puts the ball.

To indicate the position, a flag stick is put in the hole on each green. The hole is 10.8 cm in diameter and 10.2 cm in depth.

CHAPTER-14

GYMNASIUM

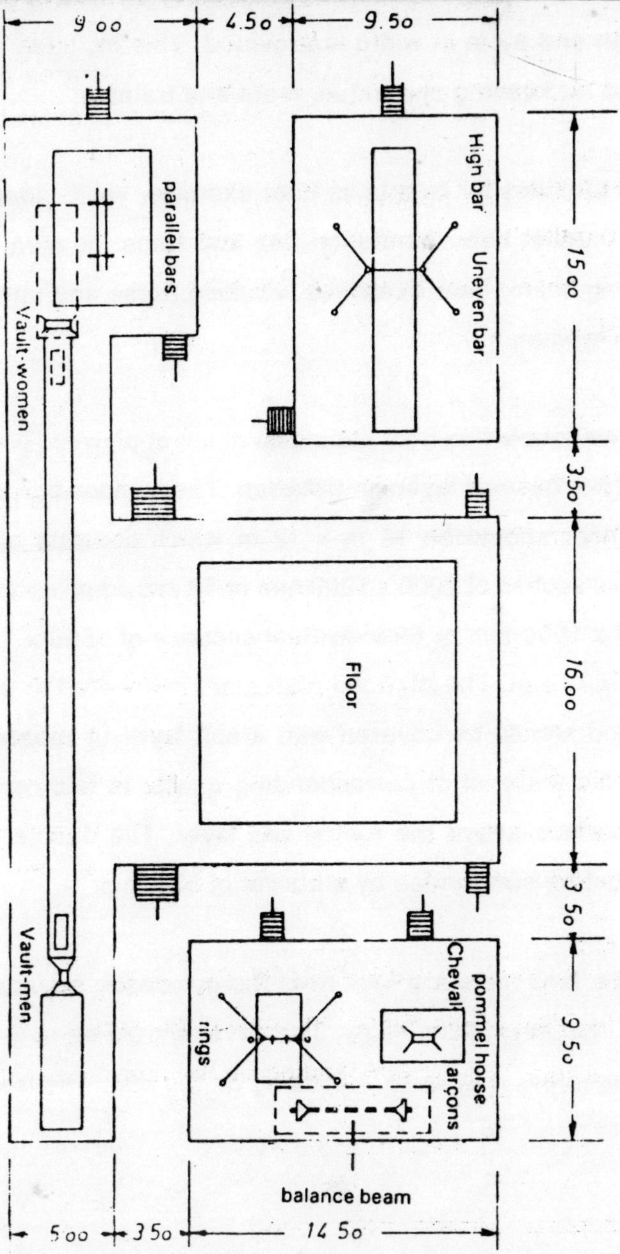

Gymnastic is a very thrilling and popular game both for men and women. It is played all over the world. The area of the field has not been specified but normally an area of 60 m. in length and 30 m in width is provided. This includes area required for keeping apparatus, mats and training.

It provides for events as floor exercise, vault, pommel horse, parallel bars, horizontal bar and rings for men and balancing beam, floor exercises, vaulting horse and uneven bars for women.

The double flex floor should be made of plywood plates on a rubber base as layers in-between. The composition area of the floor should be 12 m x 12 m which consists of 60 individual section of 2000 x 1200 mm or 48 individual sections of 2000 x 1500 mm or 68 individual sections of 1500 x 1500 mm x 50.77 mm. The plywood plates are connected to each other and should be covered with a soft layer of rubber. A carpet like material of corresponding quality is laid on the entire surface above the rubberised layer. The double flex floor must be surrounded by a border of 500 mm.

The land mats are kept near the gymnastic apparatus to save the player from injury. The cover should be non-slip and no wrinkles may arise in landing on the mat. The mats should be adopted to the ground surface of the apparatus, without any gap in between which can cause injury to the gymnast.

The size of the gymnasium hall depends upon various factors like the purpose for which the hall is used, the equipment to be kept in the hall, facilities to be provided, the financial resources and the training to be imparted. If the equipment can be placed on a podium, the area required will be less. The height of the podium should be between 0.90 - 1.10 m.

The halls are provided with facilities like bathroom, lavatories, changing rooms, store room, proper lighting, ventilation and wooden flooring arrangement. The hall of the roof should be without any projection and the roof should have sufficient height without any obstruction. The floor should be made of wood planks. Arrangements of press hooks and thrust bearing chains under the floor, should be made.

OPEN GYMNASIUM

Whenever it is not possible to construct a gymnasium, gymnastics in the open can be practiced. It is also considered preferable to practice gymnastics in the open when the climatic conditions permit. So, even when a gymnasium has been constructed, a gymnasium in the open is also provided.

Open gymnasium is normally rectangular in shape and is about 20 m x 30 m in area. The ground is hard. The wall of the gymnasium, if it is there on one side, should be used for the installation of the gymnastic apparatus. A playing field is provided adjacent to an open gymnasium. Climbing poles, climbing ropes, hanging ladders and down jump pits, as required, should be provided. Plan view of an open gymnasium with adjacent gymnasium is shown in the figure below.

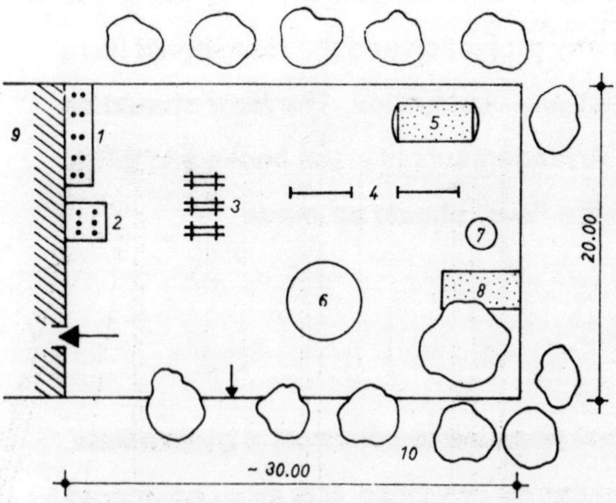

Plan view of an open gymnasium with adjacent gymnasium

1 Climbing poles
2 Climbing ropes
3 Parallel bars
4 Horizontal bar
5 Down-jump pit
6 Giant's-stride
7 Ring for putting the shot
8 Broad-jump pit
9 Gymnasium
10 Playing field

Apparatus for open gymnasium is shown in the figure below

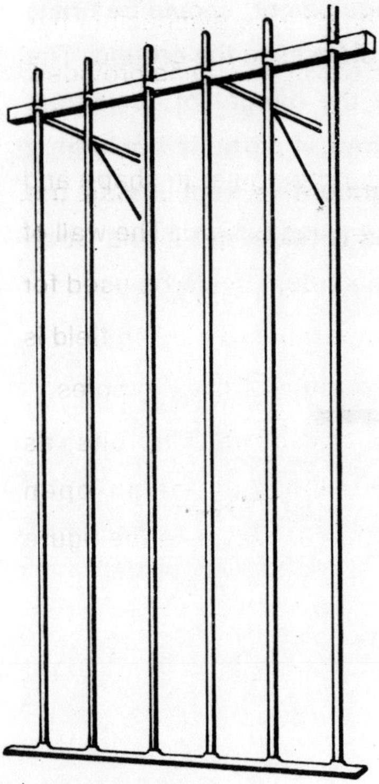

(a) Climbing poles

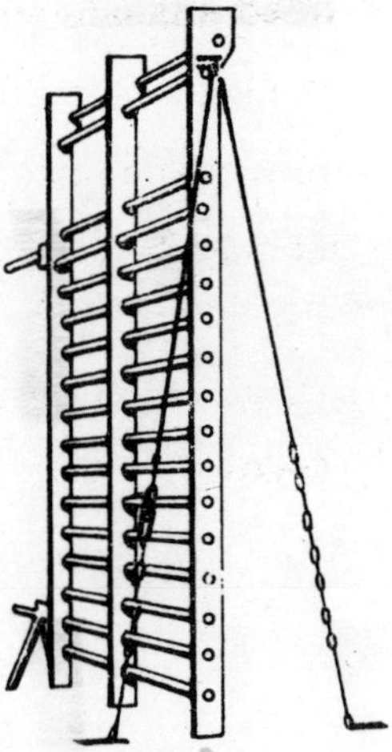

(b) Wall bars

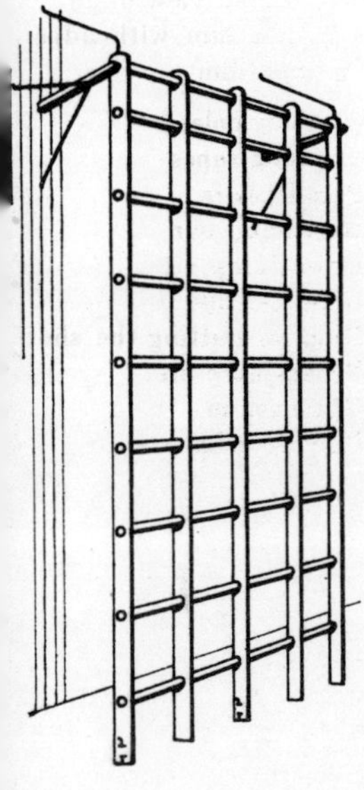

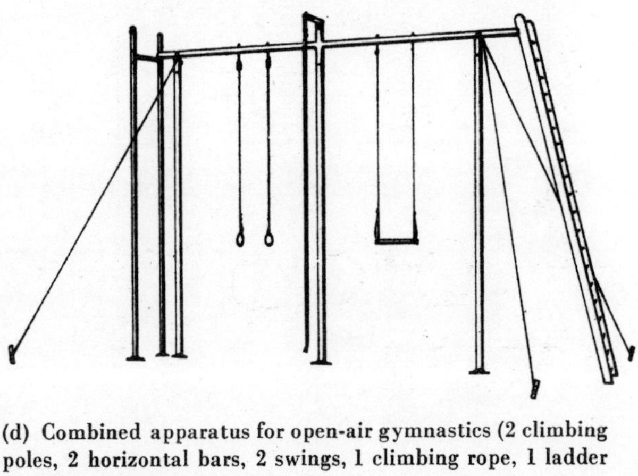

(d) Combined apparatus for open-air gymnastics (2 climbing poles, 2 horizontal bars, 2 swings, 1 climbing rope, 1 ladder

(c) Hanging ladder

Poles for the parallel bars and for the horizontal bars in addition to the above mentioned equipment, should be firmly installed. The poles are put in the sleeves in the ground. The pits are loose in order to reduce the danger of accidents. Stationary equipment is not required, if portable equipment is available. The portable equipment is kept inside the gymnasium or under a shelter and is taken out if and when need arises.

CHAPTER-15

HOCKEY

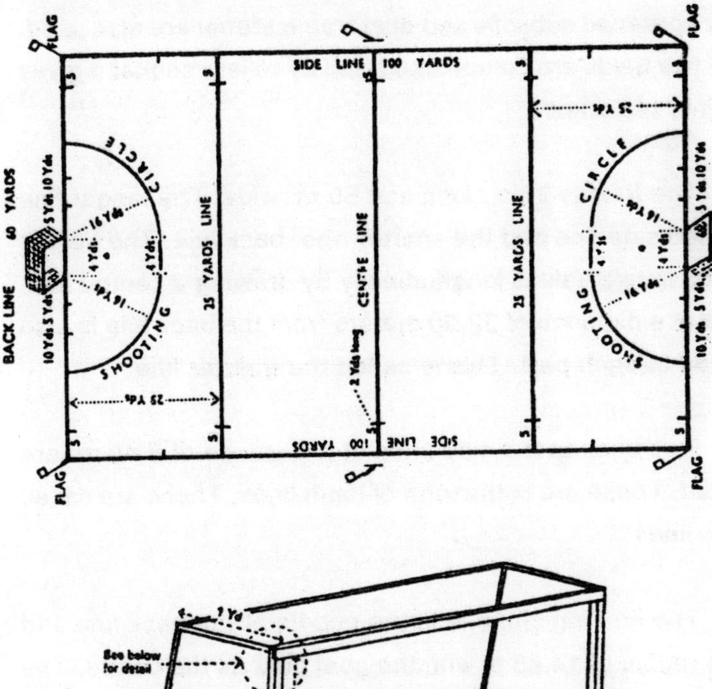

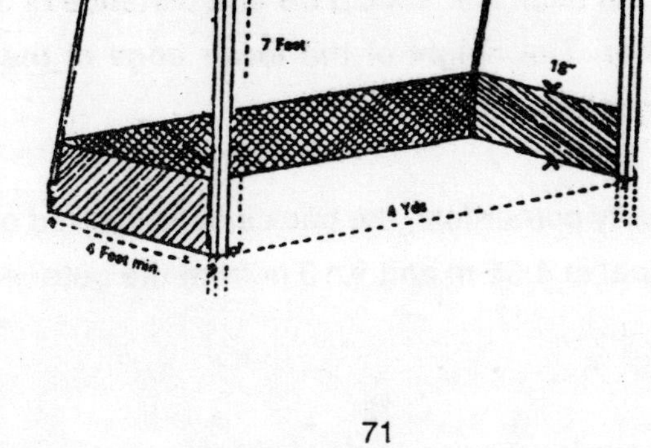

A hockey field should be perfectly plane as otherwise the ball will tend to rebound or go out of course. For hockey field, turf with close mown grass is best suited. Straws or wisps of grass impedes its play. These should be removed.

Barn floor type coat which is not hard is also used in preparing hockey fields. In some countries, sand field with finely screened subsoils and dust free material are also used. Such like fields are compressed well by rollers so that it gives required resistance.

The field is 91 m. long and 55 m. wide. The longer line is called side line and the shorter one, back line. The field is divided in two halves longitudinally by drawing a central line. A line at a distance of 22.90 meters from the back line is also marked in each part. This is called the quarter line.

Two lines to the side lines at a distance of 6.40 m. are marked. These are in the form of dash lines. These are called roll-in lines.

The striking circle is in the middle of the back line and has a radius of 14.63 m with the goal post as the centre. The two posts on the back line should be at a distance of 3.66 m from each other. The height of the lower edge of the cross bar over the goal post is 2.14 m.

For penalty corner hits, the back side is marked on both sides of the goal at 4.55 m and 9.10 m from the outer edge of the goal posts. In front of the centre of the goal, a mark is made at a distance of 4.55 m. On each side of the four corners, markings are made at a distance of 2.80 m from the corners.

At each corner of the field, flag posts are fixed. Flag posts are also fixed at the ends of the central line and the quarter lines but these are 91 cm from the side line.

The goal post is fixed at the centre of each back line touching the outer edge of the back line. Neither of the goal posts should extend beyond the cross bar. The posts and cross bars are painted white. The back boards of the goal posts are 1.25 m in length and 0.45 m in height.

CHAPTER-16

JUDO

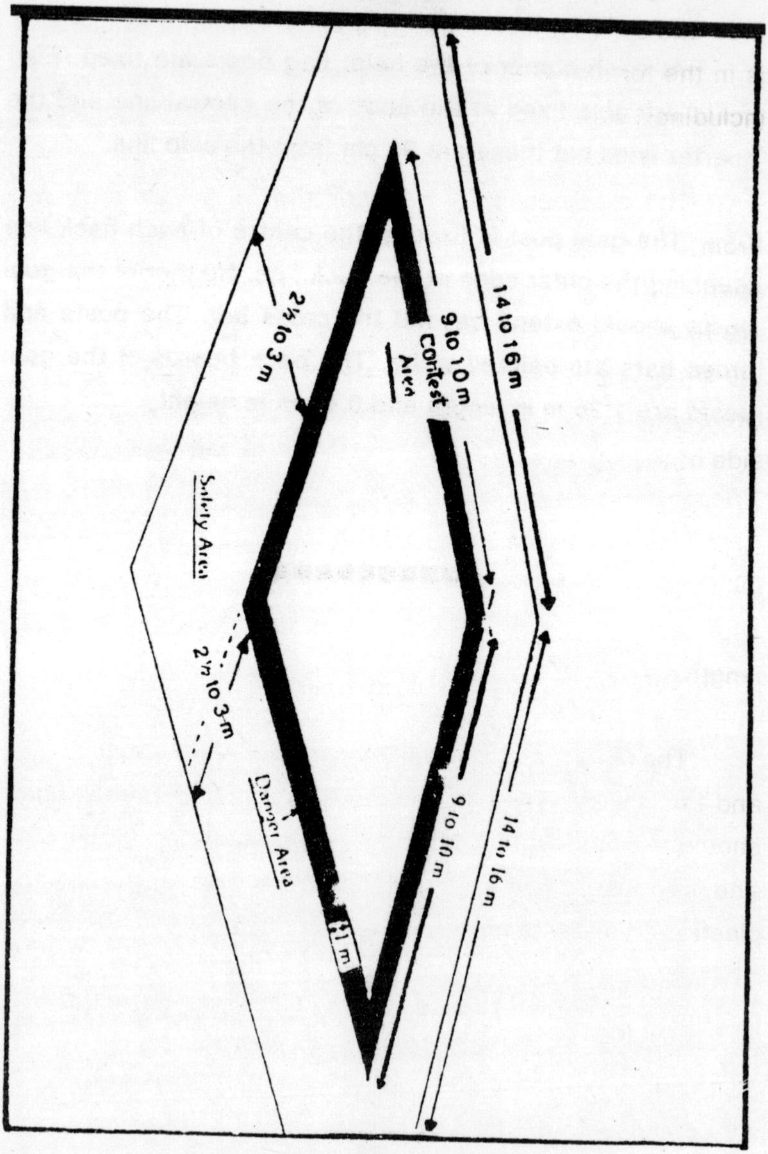

The dimension of the judo area is 14 m X 14 m. Sometimes the lengths of both sides are also increased by 2 m. The ground is covered by mats of approved material. The competition area comprises two parts, the contestant area and safety area. The contestant area is in the middle. It is in the form of a square either 9 m x 9 m or 10 m x 10 m including 1 m wide danger zone. It is generally of red colour.

The area outside the danger zone is the safety zone. From the centre of the danger zone, at a distance of 4 m apart adhesive tapes of 6 cm in width and 25 cm in length are fixed. This indicates the position of the competitors at the start and at the end of the competition. The tapes are of two colours, red and white. The right tape is at right hand side of the referee and the other on at his left side.

The game can be played on floor or a platform. The platform is made of solid wood which is elastic. It should be approximately 50 cm in height from the floor and 48 m in length and width.

The mats that cover the floor are generally 2 m in length and 1 m in width. They are made of pressed foam/straw. They should not get displaced during use, remain firm under foot and should be covered with smooth and non-slippery plasticized material of red and green colour.

CHAPTER-17

KABADDI

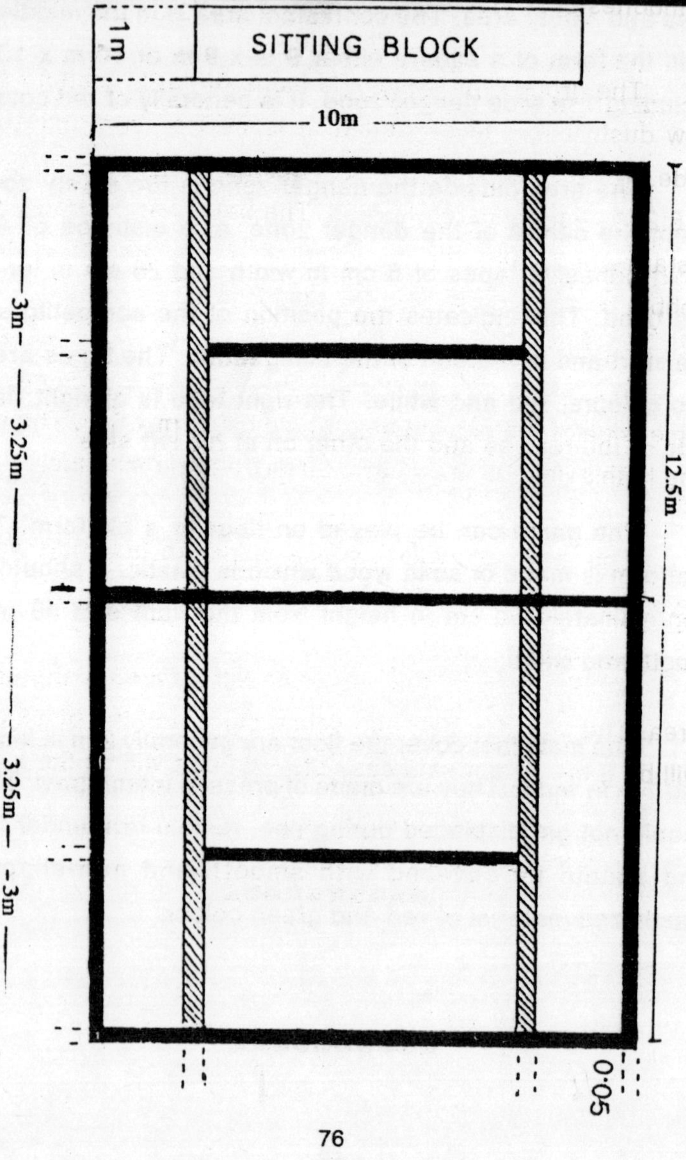

It is an ancient game played in most part of the tropical countries in Asia under different names-Kabaddi in India and Pakistan, Hududu in Bangladesh, Gudu in SriLanka and Chub in Indonesia.

The ground for kabaddi is made of earth, manure and saw dust. It is a level ground. It is 12.5 m long and 10 m wide. It is divided in two halves along its length. Each court is 6.25 m long and 10 m broad. The baulk line is drawn at a distance of 3.25 m from the mid-line. The width of the strips (lobby) on the side of the play field is 1 m.

In case of women or men below 57 kg. of weight, the dimension of the playing field would be 11 m x 8 m. The bulk line in this case is drawn at 2.50 m from the mid-line.

The maximum width of all the lines of the court would be 5 cm.

A clear area of 4 m should be left all around the game area. The distance between sitting block and the block area will be 8 m x 1 m and in case of women, it will be 6m x 1m.

CHAPTER-18

KHO - KHO

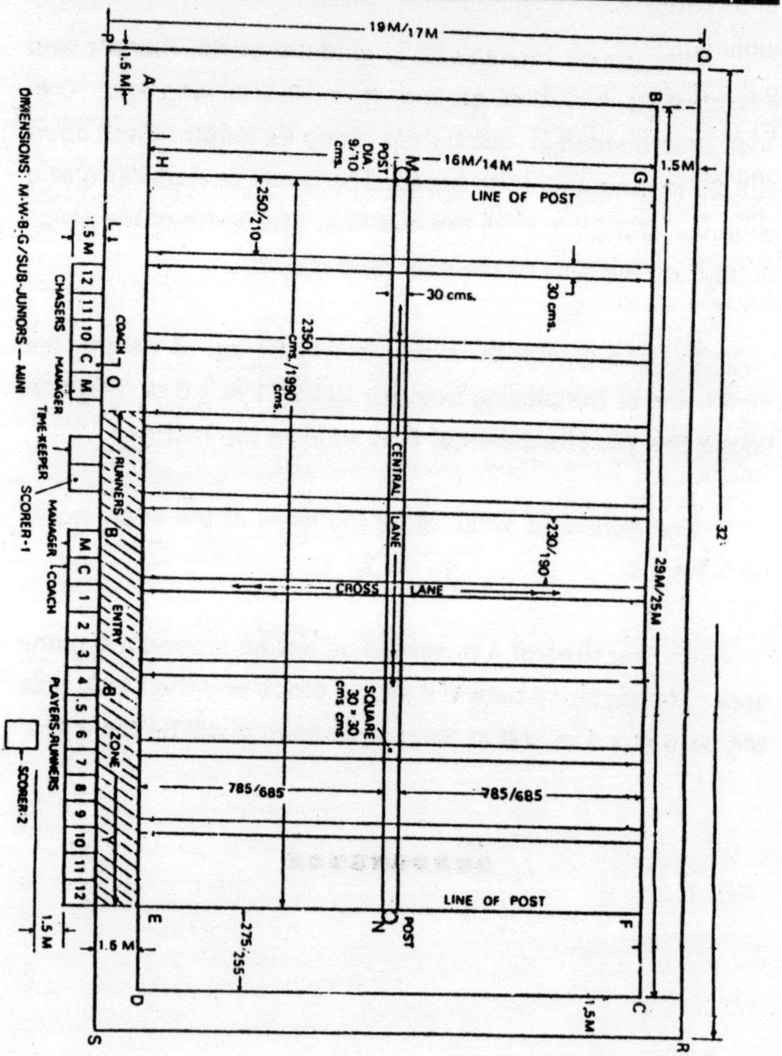

Kho-Kho is a very old game-as old as the Mahabharata days. It is very popular in India.

The field is rectangular in shape - 29 m in length and for all categories of players (men, women, boys & girls) except subjunior. For the latter category, the length will be reduced to 2.5 m and width to 14 m. The area between the post lines (EFG & F) is known as court. It is divided in two equal parts longitudinally. The length of the central line for senior and junior is 23.50 m but for sub-junior 19.90 m and width 30 cm. The cross lane which is also 30 cm. broad intersects the central lane at right angles.

The remaining portion of the field (A, B, G, H and C, D, E, F) on either side of the court are known as free zones. The width of all the lanes shown in the court shall be 3 cm.

■■■■■■■■■■■

CHAPTER-19

SOFTBALL

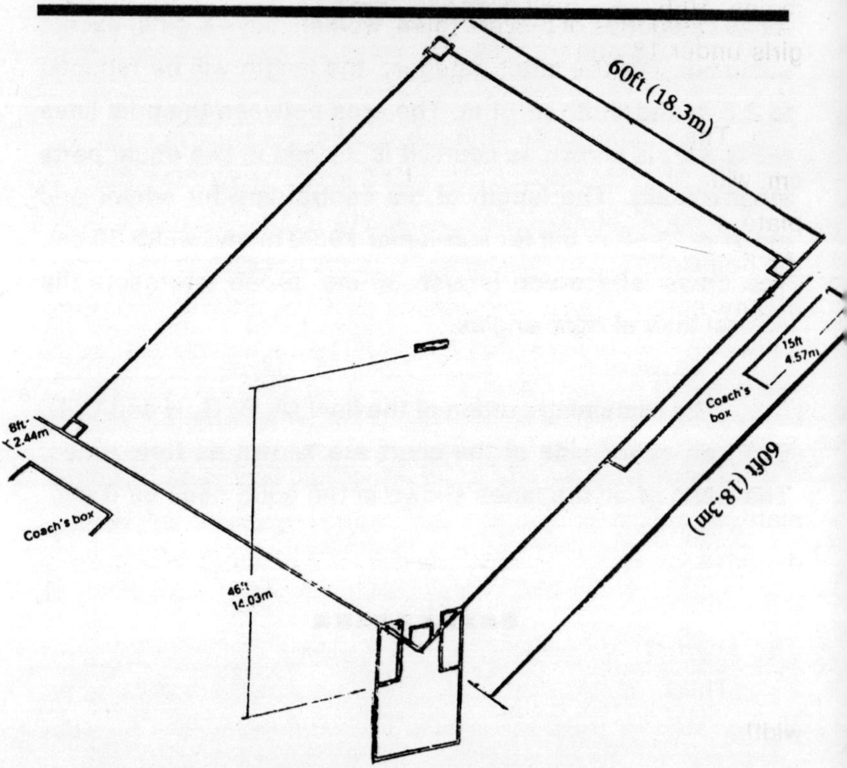

Softball resembles baseball and it originated from that game in 1888. It is also a bat and ball game.

The playing field is circular and has a radius of 70 m for men and 60 m for women from home plate to foul lines. Outside the foul line and between home plate and backslop, there is a wide area of 8 to 9 m.

It has infield and outfield. The infield which is also called diamond is a 18.3 m square. The pitching distance varies according to sex and age. It is 14 m for boys under 18 and males, 10.6 m for girls under 14 and 12 m for boys under 14, girls under 18 and for female players.

The pitcher plate is in the middle. It is 60 cm long, 15 cm. wide. A circle with a radius of 2.5 m is drawn from pitcher's plate. At the corner or base opposite to the pitcher plate is the home plate. The home plate and pitcher's plate are made of any suitable elastic material such as rubber. Starting halfway between home plate and first base, a one meter long line is drawn.

There shall be one batter's box on each side of home plate. It is 2.2 m long and 1.0 m wide. The inside line is at a distance of 15 cm from home plate. The front line drawn through the centre of home plate is 1.2 m long.

The catcher's box should be 3 m in length and 2.5 m in width.

The batters on desk circle which is near to bench or dugout is a circle of 1.5 cm radius.

The coach's box is at a distance of 2.5 m from the first and third baseline. It is outside the infield and has a dimension of 3 m x 2.5 m.

■■■■■■■■■■■

CHAPTER-20

SWIMMING

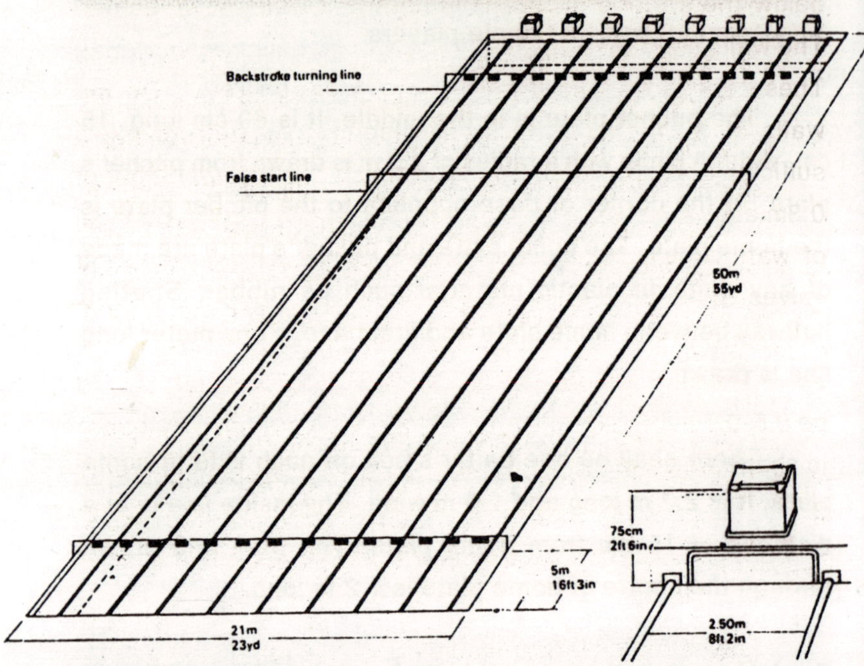

Swimming can be done either in one style or these styles can be combined.

Swimming competition is held in lines which are 50 m in length 21 m in width and 1.8 m in depth. It has eight parallel lanes each having a width of 2.5 m, thus occupying a space of 20 m. A width of 0.5m each on both sides-before the first lane and after the eighth lane, is left. The lanes are separated by ropes. At each end, these are attached to the walls by anchor brackets. At each end wall, the lane ends before a distance of 2 m with 1m cross line. On the floor of each lane, a 46 m long and 0.20 m wide lines are marked with contrast colours in its centre.

There should be tolerance of 0.3 m above and 0.8 m below the surface of water on both end walls at all points. The walls are constructed of concrete non-slippery material. These should extend 0.8 m below the water level. On the walls of the pool, gutters are placed. The gutters allow sufficient space for attachment of touch panels at a height of 0.3m above the water surface. For maintaining constant level of water, the gutters are provided with adjustable shut-off valves. The gutters are also covered with a screen.

The platform used by an athlete to make his start should be 0.5-0.7 m high from water surface. The platform is square in shape with a length of 0.5 m. These should be prominently numbered on all sides. Handgrips for backstroke should also be provided at 0.3-0.6 m above the water surface.

Arrangement, if possible, should also be made to keep the temperature of water at 22°c or 77°f. The water level should also remain constant. Inflow or outflow of water if resorted to, should not create any current, ripples or disturbance.

The use of electronic touch pad is preferred. These should be separate for each lane and should extend 30 cm above and 60 cm below the water level. These should be of bright colour.

CHAPTER-21

TABLE TENNIS

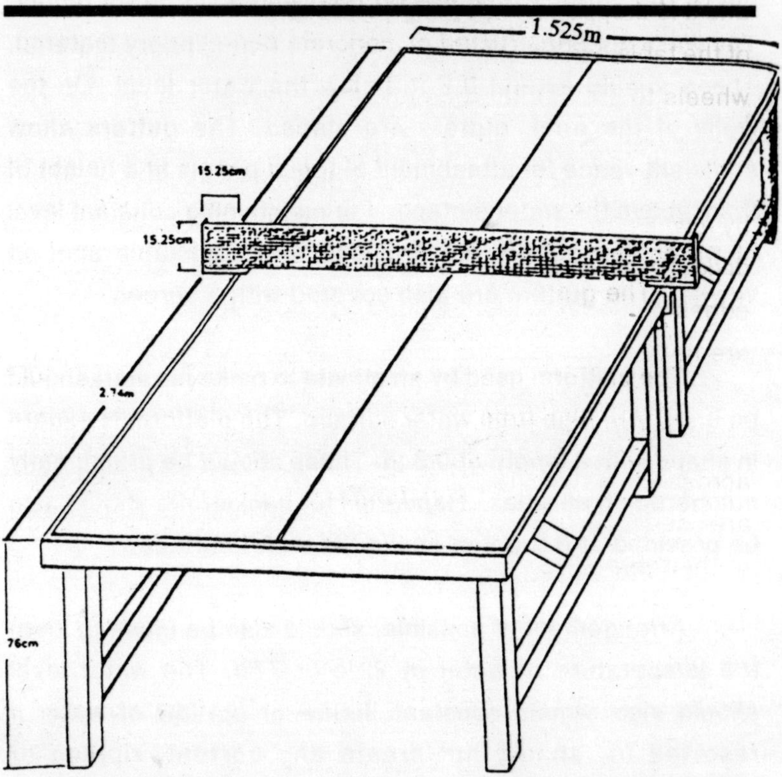

The game is played indoor in singles or doubles. The hall should be well ventilated and should have sufficient lighting facilities. The hall should have an area as required considering the number of matches to be played at a time. If a separate hall is not provided, it can be adjusted along with the other indoor games such as badminton. The floor should be non-slippery.

The game is played on a wooden table which is 2.74 m in length and 1.525 m in width and 76 cm in height. The table should be stable enough to withstand bounce or disturbances experienced during play. The surface should be such as togive a bounce of approximately 23cm if a standard T.T. ball is used and it is dropped from a height of 30cm. The supporting frame of the table can be of wood or metal. It should have supporting wheels to provide for the movement of the table.

The surface of the table is divided into two equal parts by a white line 3 mm in width. For double, each half is further divided into two halves by a white line 3 mm in width. The edges of the table are marked by 2 cm white line. The edges are not considered to be in the playing area.

The nét used has a length of 1.83 cm. It is suspended across the centre line of the table. Wooden or mental posts are used for this purpose. The height of the net from the board of the table is 15.25 cm.

CHAPTER-22

TENNIS

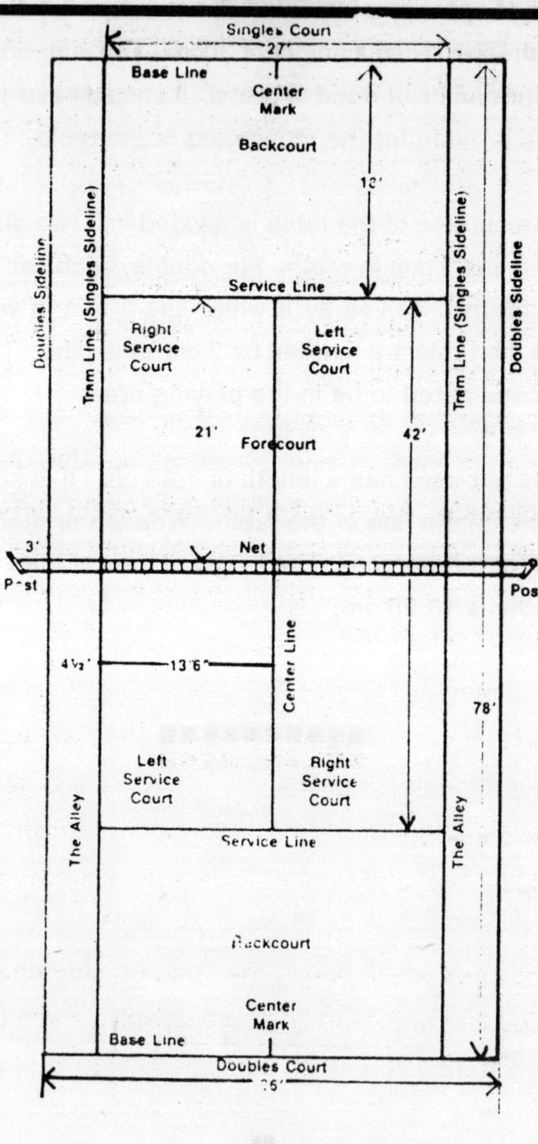

The game can be played in-doors as well as out-doors. It can be played in singles and doubles. It can also be mixed, a man and a woman form a pair.

The court can be of wood, clay, concrete, natural or artificial grass. The surface should be perfectly plane such that the ball rebounds constantly. Sometimes tennis courts have barn-floor type surface. The lower-most surface consists of natural permeable soil. The next-layer is of course slag or broken bricks, 150 to 200 cm deep. The next is the intermediate layer of slag of medium grain size or crushed clay bricks of a grain size. Its depth is 8 to 10cm. And then is the surface layer 40 to 60cm deep consisting of approximately equal quantities of brick powder, quartz sand and sandy loam. At the top is the penetrating surface water. As water is more likely to damage this surface than the hard surface, the inclination of the surface should be very small.

The court is 23.77 m in length and 10.97 m in width. It is divided in two halves longitudinally. The two long lines are the boundary lines for double. A line at a distance of 1.37 m from the boundary line for the doubles is drawn inside on either side. These are the boundary lines for the singles.

The lines which bound the court on side and base are called side line and base line respectively. From the middle line at a distance of 6.40 m, a line parallel to it on either side is drawn. It is called the surface service line. The area between the two central lines is divided by a line in two equal parts. This line is known as the surface line. The area between the service line and the base line is known as backcourt.

■■■■■■■■■■■

CHAPTER-23

VOLLEY BALL

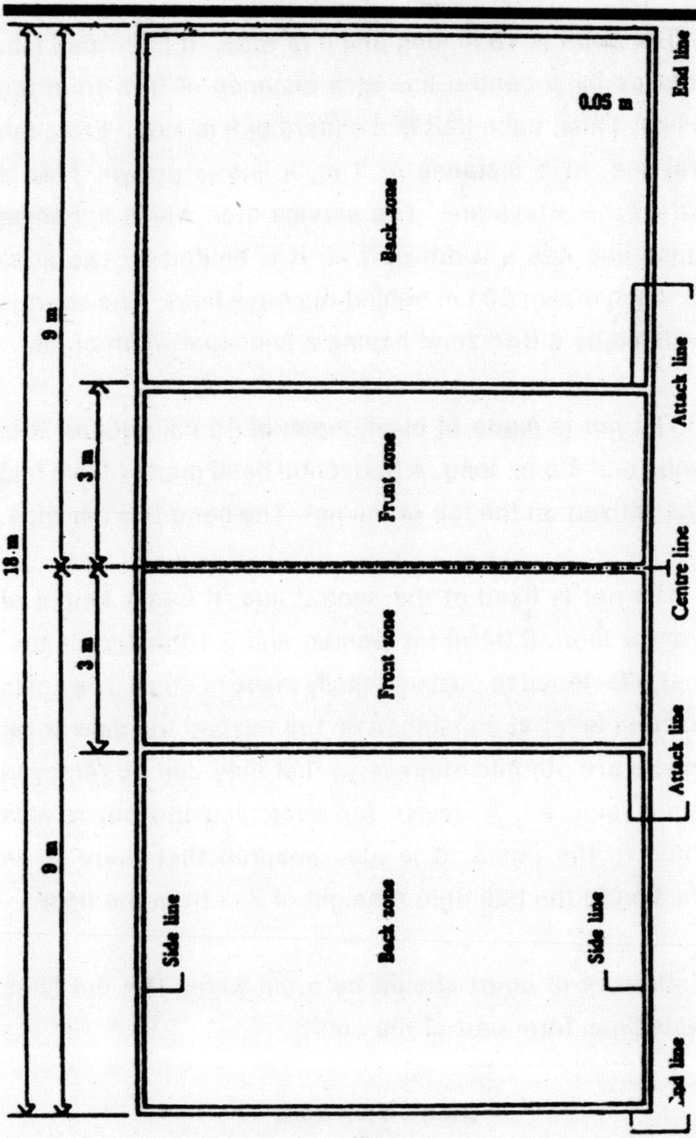

Volleyball is played on a uniform, flat and hard surface. In international competitions, the game can be played on wooden or synthetic surface.

The court is 18 m long and 9 m wide. It is divided into two halves by a central line at a distance of 9 m from the base line. Thus, each part is a square of 9 m side. From the central line, at a distance of 3 m, a line is drawn. This is known as the attack line. The service area which is behind the base line has a width of 3 m. It is limited by two lines 15cm. each drawn 20 cm behind the base lines. The court is surrounded by a free zone having a minimum width of 3m.

The net is made of black mesh of 10 cm square. It is 1 m wide and 9.5 m, long. A horizontal band made of two fold canvas is fixed on the top of the net. The band is 5 cm wide.

The net is fixed at the central line. It has a height of 2.43 m for men, 2.24 m for women and 2.10 m for juniors. The net is fastened to posts normally made of steel. The posts are fixed at least at a distance of 1 m beyond the side lines. The posts are put into sleeves so that they can be removed any time required. A devise for stretching the net is also attached to the posts. It is also ensured that there is no destruction to the ball upto a height of 7 m from the floor.

All lines of court should be 5 cm wide. The out lines and side lines form part of the court.

CHAPTER-24

WEIGHTLIFTING

The weightlifting competitions are held in halls. The hall for this purpose should be at least 16 m long and 10 m wide. The ceiling should be at a distance of 4.5 m.

It should have five wooden platforms. Of the five platforms, one should be of standard size of 4 m x 4 m and three others of 2.5 x 2.5 m. The platforms are made of seasoned wood, plastic or any other solid material. These should be covered with non-slippery material. Each plank is 6 cm in thickness. For keeping the planks together, solid iron rods of 2 cms in diameter are used.

It should have gymnastic benches with mirrors above. It should also have a changing room with wash basin and toilet facilities. It should also have lockers for keeping clothes or articles.

A disc rack for keeping weights is kept on the platform. It has a length of 80 cm and height of 35 cm at one end and 25 cm at the other end.

CHAPTER-25

WRESTLING

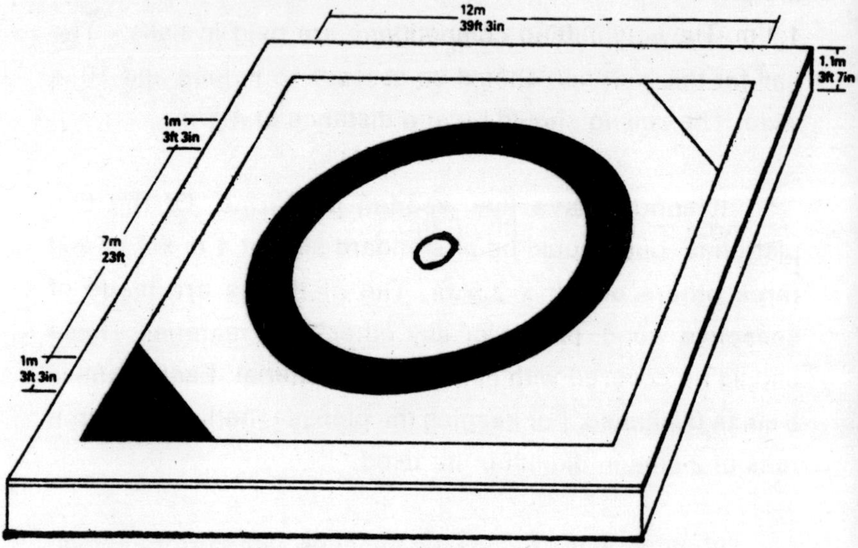

Wrestling matches are played according to weight limits. There are two types of wrestling-freestyle and greco-roman. In the later category, the competitors are not allowed to use their legs.

Both types of wrestling competitions are played on a wrestling mat which is made of rubberised or any other approved material. The total minimum mat area is 12 m x 12 m. The circular contest area in the middle is 9 m in diameter.

It is inclusive of a red band of 1 m. width running around the entire circumference. It is called passivity zone. The two diagonal corners of the mat are marked red and blue. The mat has a protection area of 1.20 m to 1.50 m. If the mats are placed on a platform, its height should not be more than 1.1 m. The total mat is covered with a synthetic/canvas cover.

CHAPTER-26

GRASS FIELD OR HARD FIELD

Normally, a grass field or a hard field is used for a particular game and there is no option. A particular game requires a particular type of field surface. In some cases, however, a grass field can be replaced by a hard field. This is done only under compelling circumstances as this will result in some draw-backs such as injuries and smoothness and continuity of play. The hard field is seldom used in place of grass field.

Grass fields and hard fields have their own advantages and disadvantages. A grass field cannot be used in wet season whereas a hard field can be used. A grass field is expensive to maintain whereas a hard field does not require any expense. A player requires boots with studs to play on grass fields but this is not necessary in case of hard field. To maintain grass in proper condition, grass field can be used for a few hours daily whereas this restriction is not applicable to hard fields.

In areas which have less rain-fall or there is deficiency of water, it is a bit difficult to maintain grass field.

A hard field has its own disadvantages. It has hard surface which can easily result in injuries to players. It easily gives rise to dust. It becomes easily heated and also reflects light of the sun more intensely. The game on a hard field cannot be so smooth and continuous as in the case of grass field. A hard field is also not so pleasing to look at.

As such, for large fields, grass field is best suited and is laid down for use in competitions. In case of small-scale games such as basket-ball, volley-ball etc. no such condition is laid down.

Where sports facilities provide for a number of games, the main field may be a grass field and playing fields for secondary games may be hard. Playing fields for training purpose should be hard as it can withstand greater use.

In schools, the play-ground should be grassy as well as hard so that these could be used according to weather conditions.

Before taking a decision about setting up of a grass field or a hard field, all the factors should be given due consideration.

GRASSFIELDS

When laying down a grass field, attention has to be paid to many factors. It should be free from weeds. It should be of the same density and colour. The grass should be of good quality and properly grown so that it can withstand wear by games. Much depends on the composition and thickness of the soil and its moisture contact. It not only calls for experience in horticulture but special knowledge and experience in laying grassfields. If a grass field is properly prepared and well looked after, it can last for years.

SOIL COMPOSITION

Attention has to be paid to the soil composition of the field. It should consist of 50% fine sand and coarse silt, 10% gravel and coarse sand, 20% settling components and 20% humus. The subsoil should be richer in mineral and the top layer should have exceedingly well bacterial life.

There are five different types of soils-sandy soil, clay soil, loam soil, humus soil and moor soil. A change can be made from one soil to another according to requirement and weather conditions. It is necessary to know the composition, properties and methods of improvement of these soils.

Sandy soil consists of quartz particles and the amount of settling components is too small. On the other hand, clay soil consists of small quantity of sand and its amount of settling components is too big. Loam soil is a mixture of clay, sand and humus. Humus soil has much humus with an acid reaction. Moor soil is a kind of humus soil.

Sandy soil does not form crumbs easily and has poor water retention capability. It also becomes dry quickly. On the other hand, the clay soil is tough, water passes through with difficulty and crumbs are not formed. Loam soil is a fertile soil and can contain water. Humus soil is wet in nature, cold and has larger quantity of nitrogen. Moor soil contains much water, is cold and acidic.

Improvement in sandy soil can be made by use of manure, peat and lime. Clay soil is improved by adding manure, woodashes, fine sand, coke fines, phosphorous and humus. In loam soil, a distinction is made between loamy sandy soil and sand of loamy soil and improvement is to be made accordingly. In humus soil or moor soil, it might be necessary to add fine sand, lime, potash and phosphoric acid.

SOIL IMPROVEMENT

Crumbs allow for much more free movement of air and rich bacterial life. This is the requirement of a good soil. Air circulation is not possible if the soil particles adhere together too closely or in a way cemented together.

The soil can be improved by mechanical and chemical means.

If the soil is heavy, it can be improved by harrowing and then loosened by adding coarse or coke fines or a mixture of straw manure and compost. If the soil is light, any cohesive matter, manure and compost are added. If the soil is wet, it is drained.

Chemically, the soil can be improved by the addition of nitrogen, phosphorous and potash. Soil normally lacks nitrogen. The addition of nitrogen is necessary for the growth and colour of the grass. Phosphorous is necessary for rapid growth of roots. Potash is necessary to protect the grass from various diseases caused by fungi.

For improvement of soil, manures and fertilizers are added, the composition of which must be known. Manures are normally of six types-compost earth, compost of leaves, liquid manure, sewage sludge, horse dung and cow dung. Artificial fertilizers are mostly of five types-chile nitre, soot, ammonium sulphate, thomas meal and superphosphate. Of the manures, the sewage sludge has highest amount of nitrogen (7.5 units) and phosphorous (3 units). The compost of leaves comes next to sewage sludge in the content of nitrogen-it is nearly half. The maximum amount of potash is contained in liquid manure and next come compost earth and compost of leaves. It, however, contains a negligible amount of phosphorous.

It is necessary to have certain consideration in the use of manures. Liquid manure should be used after mixing it with dunghill. Sewage sludge should not be used where the soil is acidic. Cow-dung is used not for top dressing but only for improvement of soil.

Of the artificial fertilizers, ammonium sulphate contains the highest amount of nitrogen (21 units) and the next comes chile nitrate (18 units). These two fertilizers do not contain any phosphorous or potash. Next comes soot which contains 4 units of nitrogen. Soot contains maximum amount of potash (1.5 units) but no phosphorus. Super phosphate contains the maximum amount of phosphorous (18 units) and then comes thomas meal (16 units). Both these fertilizers do not contain any nitrogen or potash. Ammonium sulphate is the best grass fertilizer. Soot is used to combat fungai diseases. Thomas meal is used where there is deficiency of lime in the soil.

For addition of lime certain considerations are necessary. Mostly soil contains enough of lime. Where it is too much, the condition can be improved by slow addition of ammonium sulphate. Where the soil is acidic, lime is added to improve the condition of the soil.

To know the contents of a soil and how these can be remedied, it is necessary to send the soil to any agricultural consultation service for testing. It will avoid much botheration and expenses later.

CONSTRUCTION OF GRASS FIELDS

If the soil is such that it does not soak water easily, a good drainage system has to be installed. It consists of sub-drains and collecting drains. The sub-drains consist of perforated pipes ranging in diameter from 3 cm to 10 cm depending upon the amount of water to be drained. The pipes are laid below the ground at a distance of about 40 to 50 cm below the surface. The pipes rest on a layer of crushed clay bricks or rock in which is filled a layer of gravel or slag. The surface water runs into these crushed clay bricks or rocks.

The collecting drains are thicker than the sub-drain pipes and they take the water from the sub-drains to the municipal drainage system. It should be ensured that the level of the sub-drains and collecting drains is such that there is no difficulty in the flow of water to municipal drainage system otherwise a pump will have to be installed to serve this purpose.

Sometimes, it may happen that there is no municipal drainage system or if it is, it is far off. Special soaking pots will then have to be constructed which many take the water to water-bearing layer of the soil.

If there is heavy rainfall, small pools of dirty water will form. The water cannot easily pour down into the drainage system. So to prevent the formation of these puddles and to run off the surface water, the playing fields are elevated at some places to enable the water to flow to the sides. To prevent washing off the soil, the elevation should be small. The main inclination should be across the field.

The degree of slope depends on the local conditions- the extent and intensity of rainfall, the nature of soil, and the length of the field. If the extent and intensity of rainfall is high, the slope will be a bit on the higher side. If the nature of the soil is such that water can pass through it easily and it can absorb this water, the slope can be less. The soil can also be made more absorbent. A layer of coarse sand, small stones or any other absorbent material is properly laid in right proportion in the sub-soil. The sub-soil should be smooth and plane. The side soil should also be made loose by harrowing. The length of the field is also taken into consideration in deciding the extent of slope. The greater the field the lessen can be the slope.

The top soil should be laid in layers and each layer should be compact. It may also require harrowing. The top-most layer should be quite stable so that no foot mark is left over it.

SOWING OF GRASS

The soil has also to be conditioned with a view to proper growth of grass. Some fertilizers may be mixed in the soil. All types of grasses cannot be suitable for laying a turf. Only a few types of grass seeds can be used and the soil has to be conditioned considering the nature of grass to be cultivated. The grass seeds are also mixed considering the variations in climate. The grass should not be able to retain too much water. The grass should also not be too dry or too soft. It should not be capable of giving way for the growth of other plants.

A proper quantity of a mixture of different seeds in proper proportion should be used. The ground is sown by hand and all the area should be properly and uniformly covered. The sown area should be then properly covered with a thin layer of soil. When the grass is grown, it is cut by means of a scythe and if there is any foreign plant, it is removed. Thereafter, mowing is done at regular interval of time.

SPRINKLING AND IRRIGATION

Provision of adequate irrigation facilities and suitable lawn-sprinkler system are very important for maintenance of grass, particularly in dry weather. The underground water system should be installed along the boundaries of the playing ground. The hydrands should be at intervals so that all the ground can be reached and irrigated properly. An overheal irrigation installation is also available which can advantageously be used for this purpose. It is a self-travelling spray-line irrigator. It ensures uniform watering and eliminates the need for going into the water-soaked turf. Ordinary sprinklers can also be used to provide water within their reach.

In providing the irrigation facilities, the water pressure, the diameter of the pipes and the extent of ground to be fertilized are to be considered. The hose method is not suitable because it does not provide for even distribution of water.

It is advisable not to use too much water to water the ground at a time bit to provide reasonable water at reasonable interval of time in accordance with the weather. This should be done when the water content of the ground decreases considerably but not to the extent of making it hard. In the latter case, water will not be able to soak the ground. If more water is provided to the ground than that is necessary, it will promote fungi and cause fungi causing diseases.

The water from the main should not be spread directly on the grass but it should be allowed to attain the atmospheric temperature by directing it upwards in the air. The quantity of water required depends on the nature of the soil and the climatic conditions. The sandy soils require more water than the heavy soils.

The irrigation system also ensures, equilable distribution of fertilizers.

CULTIVATION OF GRASS FIELDS

It should be ensured that the grass is short as if to provide a mat to play on and not long enough to hide small plants. For this purpose the grass should be mown regularly.

Weeds should be cut along with their roots. The holes thus created should be fitted with earth mixed with fertilizers and grass seeds. If there are many weeds, this method might not be suitable. Certain chemicals which kill only such like plants should be used. The weeds should be cut or treated just when they come out of the earth. The detailed information about the use of the chemicals is provided by the manufacturers. If the field is continuously in use, grass in the holes cannot grow. In that case, holes should be cut so that turf sods can be put. Grass should, therefore, be grown over a large field so that it can be used for this purpose.

To keep the turf in good condition, the field should not be utilized for more than 2 or 3 hours daily. Whenever the play field is wet even slightly due to rain, irrigation or frost, it should not be used. There should also be a spell of rest for the grass field as if during raining seasons. During this period, hard fields can be used.

When the grass is cut, it is deprived of certain nutritive matter. So it must be replenished with fertilizers. Thus, the growth of grass would be satisfactory. Manures or fertilizers should be spread during the period of growth of the grass or else it will force the grass to grow weakening its resistance power. A number of fertilizers can be used. These are usually combined to provide proper nutrition to the soil. Most important of these fertilizers are ammonium sulphate, superphosphate and potash. They can be mixed in proper proportion say 2 : 4 : 1 respectively for one square meter. The strength of these fertilizers should also be taken into consideration.

The surface is aerated by means of a harrow before fertilizers are put. special rolls for this purpose are available. To prevent the surface from being hard, the turf should not be rolled too frequently.

Coarse sand should be spread over hard soil from time to time to improve its surface. In case of light soils, a layer of loose earth or compost is laid.

Various types of plant and insect pests destroy grass. These can be destroyed by the application of certain chemicals and use of certain fertilizers. In addition to these, attention should be paid to certain factors to prevent diseases due to fungi. These include, as little as possible watering of the ground, quick drainage of surface water, sufficient circulation of air above the turf, aeration of hard soils, addition of sufficient amount of phosphate and potash fertilizers, improvement of heavy soils and reducing the content of lime in the soil, if it is too high.

HARD FIELDS

Hard fields are of different types. These depend upon the nature of material used. The details of the material normally used for hard fields are given in the table below.

Base course	Intermediate layer	Wearig course	
		Cohesive matter	Filling Material
Broken concrete	Burnt clay chippings	Sandy loam	Powdered bricks
Broken Bricks	Crushed stones (natural stones)	Tuff sand	Sand
Natural stones		Clay containing silt	Gravel of 4 to 12 mm grain size
Coarse slag	Granulated slag	Cinders	Fine slag
	Aggregate of crushed concrete	Humus	

BARN-FLOOR TYPE SURFACINGS

Sometimes soil does not allow water to penetrate easily. In that case, certain steps have to be taken to prepare the ground. First proper drinage system is arranged. The base course is then built. This is done by removing a layer of earth of about 25 to 35 cm thickness. Broken bricks having a thickness of about 15 to 20 cm are then placed. On this, a layer of burnt clay chips or slag of thickness about 10 cm is made. The surface or top layer which normally wears out is made up of a mixture of various materials which can withstand high stress and in which water can penetrate. This material is spread to a thickness of about 5 cm. This is done by skimming and rolling. Brick powder or quartz sand is then spread over this layer.

This type of surfacing is suitable for most of the games but special consideration has to be given in preparing ground for certain games as in the case of tennis court. In a tennis court, a constant rebound of the ball has to be ensured. For this purpose an intermediate layer of slag of medium grain size or crushed clay brick has to be laid below the surface layer.

The field prepared should be slightly inclined. As barn-floor type surface is more liable to damages by action of water, the inclination should be very small.

SAND SURFACINGS

Sand surfacing is a type of make-shift arrangement. It has to be attended to after every match. It cannot withstand high pressure and has to be smoothed and rolled. It also provides poor footing, easy formation of dust and growth of weeds. The sand surfacing does not require any base.

The downmost layer is the natural soil which is permeable and on this, a layer of quartz sand with an addition of loam is laid.

Slag surface has a little advantage over the sand surface. It contains cohesive matter and is finally grained.

BITUMENOUS SURFACINGS

This type of surfacing is popular for the reason that it has a long life, is free from dust and requires no maintenance. This also increases the speed of the ball and is, therefore, more suitable for ball games.

It is, however, a little hard but this disadvantage is off-set by mixing certain materials. The foundation course is of cinder type and on this is laid an intermediate course of slag of about 10 cm thickness. This improves the elasticity of the top surface.

There is also one binder coat consisting of slag bound together by means of asphalt bitumen red emulsion. On this is laid a thick layer of fine grain and bitumen cemented together. On this is placed fine sand bounded by bitumen. To improve the elasticity of the surface, rubber particles are added to this mixture. This also improves the foothold.

Light colour reflects less solar heat than dark colour. In order to limit the temperature, light colour materials are preferred in construction of the field.

As the bitumenous surface does not absorb water, it requires a good drainage system. Inlet shafts should conduct the water quickly. The fields have a slight tilt towards the outside.

As the bitumenous surfaces are liable to become too hot in sunshine, they are not recommended. However, school grounds, tennis and basket-ball courts are made of this surface.

MAINTENANCE OF HARD FIELDS

Hard fields require very much less maintenance than grassfields. The top layer should be swept from time to time and new brick powder or quartz should be spread. Water should be spread on the field to bind the dust particles. A lawn sprinkler in case of large fields and a hose in case of small fields can be used. Particular care in this respect should be taken during hot weather and for matches when the field is exposed to stress.

Whenever the ground is exposed to high stresses, the field should be skimmed and then rolled. Even otherwise, the top layer should be renewed say every two years with fresh material. If it is simply repaired, it will one day become thick and too soft.

It is not considered advisable to roll the surfaces which exist for a long time. They should be simply sprinkled with water.

Special care is required in case of tennis court. Its surface is completely renewed say after every 6 years as it will no longer allow water to penetrate.

MARKING THE PLAYING FIELDS

Normally, lines of all sports fields are of 5 cm. If there is to be any difference, it is specifically mentioned.

While chalk or lime is used for this purpose, glue can be added to increase its durability. Liquid paint can also be used. This is particularly used in case of tennis courts. Permanent shaped markings are not advisable because these are likely to cause injuries.

Before marking, the lines are determined precisely with the help of steel tape measure. Guide cords are stretched to indicate the position of the lines. The important points are preferably marked with the help of nails.

The staff of the flags should have a minimum length of 1.70 m and a diameter of 3 cm. This saves the falling players from sustaining serious injuries. The flag staff is pointed at the lower end to drive it into the ground. The boundary flags are placed at certain distance from the side lines.

In the case of goal posts and net posts, there is a difference. These are not directly driven into the ground as it is necessary to change these posts from time to time. These are put in sleeve, which are driven into the ground. The sleeves are permanently driven. These consist of metal or concrete and are covered when not in use to prevent dust from getting in. The depth of the sleeve depends on the length and thickness of the poles. The poles are not put upto the bottom of the sleeve but a few cms above it on a cross pin. In order to avoid movement of the poles, these are locked by means of wedges. A hole is provided at the bottom of the sleeve for drainage of rain water.

In cases, where the poles have to bear much strain as in the case of volley-ball, basket-ball and football, the supports are provide with a permanent and firm foundation. Sometimes, additional steel support is also provided. If the poles are of portable type, they are kept in position by the application of ballast.

In schools and colleges and for training purposes, it is not necessary to make this provision. Simply, poles can be used.

TRAINING FIELDS, MULTI-PURPOSES SPORTS FACILITIES AND TRAINING EQUIPMENT

If a grass field is required for training, a supplementary grass field rather than the main grass field should be used for the purpose. A grass field is, however, not necessary for the purpose of training. The training requirements can very well be met on a hard field.

For football and handball training, a wall is erected and the goal area is divided into about 10 equal rectangles to enable the player to hit at the directed spot. To enable practice of hard work, a cross bar is erected. Two balls are tied to a string on either side of the cross bar. The string moves on the pullies fixed on the crossbar.

For tennis training, a wall is also provided and an area equal to that of the tennis court is also marked. The ground in front of the wall should be sufficiently hard to enable the ball to rebound properly.

For small-field games, multi-purpose sport facilities are provided. Markings on the ground should be made with care, so that they do not get mixed up in case of several games.

It is advisable to provide training facilities at a field not close to the main ground so that these can go on uninterrupted.

■■■■■■■■■■■

CHAPTER-27

DESIGN OF SMALL STADIUM

Important sports events are also sometimes played in villages and towns. It is, therefore, natural for them to have desire for a stadium to enable them to watch these events favorably. Stadium include open playing in the middle with rows of seats around. The rows of seats rise behind and above each other enabling large number of people to sit and enjoy seeing the game comfortably. This seating arrangement called tier system becomes necessary when the number of spectators is 700 or more. The size of a stadium depends on the number of spectators likely to witness the game. When the number is less than that, the sports grounds are surrounded by barriers to provide standing space for the spectators without causing any distraction to the players.

Design and construction depends on the money available for the purpose, number of workmen required and easily available and the building material readily available.

At the centre of the stadium is the playing field which caters for a large number of sports in which the local people are normally interested. It should also have a running track. If local people are interested in a particular game or sport, only then arrangement for it should be made. All the other installations supplementary to the stadium are provided on these very principles.

ARRANGEMENT OF TIERS FOR THE AUDIENCE

The raised structure for the spectators to sit or stand below each other is called tiers. The arrangement of tiers vary greatly and on this depends the appearance of a stadium.

Tiers should be constructed in such a way as to provide the spectators an unobstructed view of the game from various places and they should feel comfortable. A stadium should provide seating arrangement for a maximum number of people.

A large number of building materials are available for construction. It can be made of steel, reinforced concrete etc. in case of large scale stadia. A small stadium can be made by filling or excavation of earth. The terrace providing for standing room should be 0.40 m one above the other and there should be five or six such tiers. The maximum height of the tier should be 2.00 m. The width of the tier should be 0.80 m. There should be 1 m space each in front of the tiers and at the back of the last tier. The terraces in an earth fill embankment should be 5 m. in length and it should have a slope such that its maximum height is .50 m.

The factors governing the arrangement of tiers are:-

(a) The number of expected spectators,

(b) The altitude of the sun,

(c) The climatic conditions,

(d) The range of vision,

(e) The architectural conception.

The number of spectators vary from place to place. It depends on the population of the village or town, the nature of interest of people in these events and the importance of competitions held. The number of expected spectators can be roughly calculated on this basis. As the interest of the people of the area increases in sports, or the population of the area increases, the requirement of area for sports will increase. These factors have also to be kept in mind while catering for the area required for the stadium. Since the standing room required for one person is 0.2 m² and that for one seat is 0.4 m², the total area required for tiers can be easily calculated. The tiers can be arranged round the whole or only along one or both sides of the playground. The areas required for stairs, paths and roads for traffic have also to calculated and added. The designs of tiers can be possibly of one of these types.

For the purpose of good visibility, it is advisable to arrange the auditorium on the two longitudinal sides. Visibility will be impaired because the distance from the curves to the scene of action will be large. Instead of straight rows, it will be better if the seats on the long sides are curved. It will provide better visibility towards the right and the left.

The architect can make a design as to admit natural scenery in the stadium. He can also make a design as to exclude natural scenery and make best use of the limited area available.

While designing the arrangement of tiers, it has also to be kept in mind that the sun does not strike the eyes of the spectators directly. If possible, it should also be ensured that the mirror does not strike the faces of the spectators.

The movement of the players can be seen clearly upto about 160 m. Beyond this limit, their movement cannot be observed clearly. So the size of the stadium should not be of large dimensions.

When the nature of the game is such, as in the case of boxing and judo, where the smaller movements are to be seen, the maximum distance should be 50 m. otherwise the game cannot be observed properly.

Tennis or basket-ball courts or such like other small playing fields are also provided with tiers, usually in the form of stands.

STANDING-ROOM AND SEATS FOR THE AUDIENCE

It is always preferable to provide seating arrangement for as many spectators as possible. Standing-room for the spectators may be necessary but this to some extent diverts the attention of the spectators. If the seats are full and spectators rush for the standing seats, it will add to the confusion. It can also discourage the visitors to witness the sport events.

A seat is to have a width of 50 cm and a depth of approx. 70 cm. For standing room, a width of 50 cms and a depth of 40 cm is required for one person.

To enable all the spectators to have a good view of the game, the tiers should be arranged in steps in a ratio of 1 : 2. If the stands have inclined plane with inclination more than 10 per cent, it becomes uncomfortable. This particularly applies to standing-room.

Tiers in the form of steps to stand upon should be for 1 to 3 persons one behind the other. When seats are provided, one tier should be made for one row of seats only.

The designs of the terraces according to requirement are shown in the figures below.

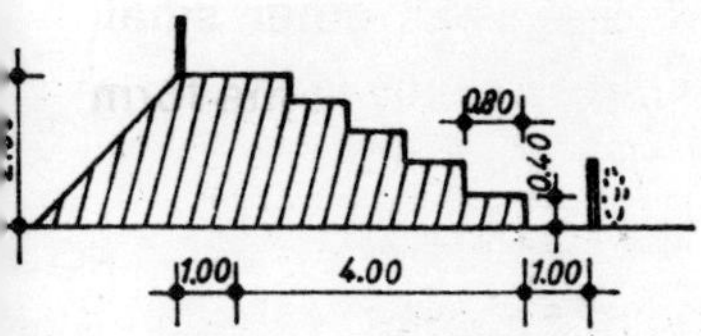

Terraces providing tanding-room

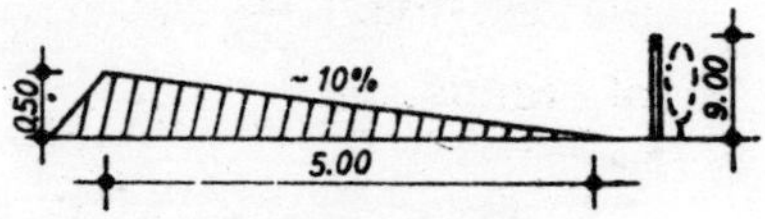

Terraces in an earth fill embankment

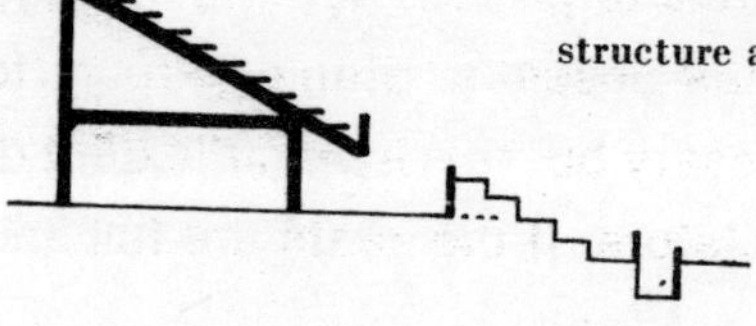

Grand stand with super-structure and excavated terraces

Particularly in the case of small-sized and medium-sized sport grounds, visibility is good, if the arrangement of the auditorium is as shown in fig. above. The curved tiers improve the visibility.

If the structure is high with many tiers, it should not be linear but should have a parabolic curve.

In this way, the visibility of the spectators on the upper tiers will improve.

In order to make the seats weather-resistant, these are made of plywood mixed with synthetic resin or plastic. Synthetic resin and plastic are weather-resistant. Provision for draining of rain water from the seats have also to be made. The seats have normally no back-rest.

■■■■■■■■■■■

CHAPTER-28

HANDLING THE TRAFFIC

The traffic of a stadium can be classified in two categories-Interior and Exterior. The traffic upto the back of the enclosure is exterior traffic and this includes the approach roads, parking places and entrances. The interior traffic is handled to make the spectators reach their seats easily.

HANDLING THE INTERIOR TRAFFIC

The visitors are to be shown the shortest distance to their seats. The roads and paths inside the stadium should be marked clearly so that a few stewards are required to guide the visitors to their seats and to enable them to leave the stadium comfortably after the sport is over.

The arrangement is not difficult in the case of small stadium. The paths usually run along the embankment. In the case of large stadium, the paths to the lower tiers are through tunnels.

Ramps are not normally provided to afford access to the tiers. The requirement is met by a flight of stairs. The steps of the stairs should not be smaller than 25 cm and its height should not be longer than 19 cm. The stairs should preferably be straight. The landings are arranged every 5 m in rise. Handrails are provided to the stairs and landings for grasping as a support.

The whole stadium should be divided into blocks. These blocks should have separate approaches. The blocks should neither be too small or too big. Normally each blockshould have a capacity for roughly 1.000 people.

The layout of the approach may be as shown in the figure below. It shows the main entrance, primary paths, secondary paths and the seats.

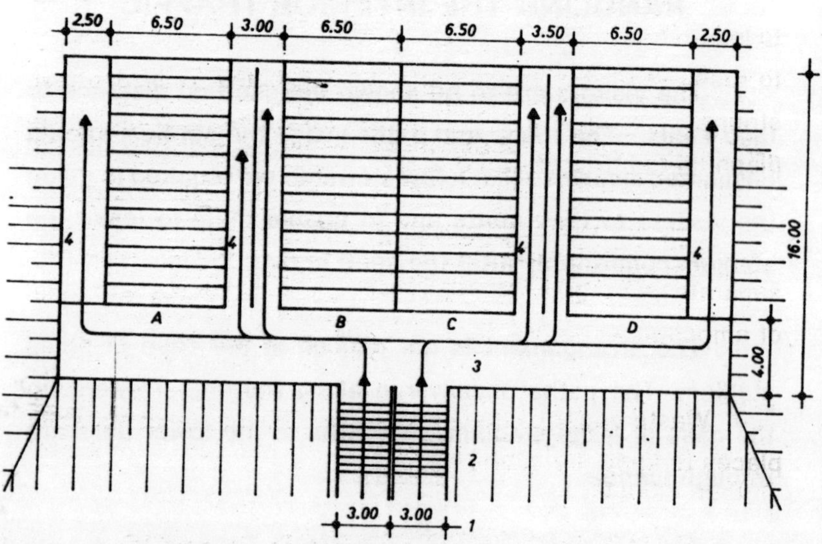

Fig. 87 Approach of the spectators on primary and secondary paths to their seats

A Block A 260 spectators (20 rows, 13 spectators each)
B Block B 260 spectators (20 rows, 13 spectators each)
C Block C 260 spectators (20 rows, 13 spectators each)
D Block D 260 spectators (20 rows, 13 spectators each)

total 1,040 spectators

The main entrance is in the middle of the embankment of the stadium and at one end of the public transport. It should be wide enough approx. 3 m to allow easy entry. The main entrance has two passages, one leading to the right and the other to the left. These passages are about 2.5 m wide and lead to the fore-courts in front of the stairs. These fore-courts are about 1.5 m wide. These should not allow crowding in front of the stairs.

There are four passages to the courts. Their width ranges from 2.50 m to 3.50 m.

Arrangement should be made to enable the spectators to leave the stadium in about 10 minutes. The spectators try to rush out of the stadium and are subjected to the highest strains. This should, therefore, be taken into account while planning the flow of traffic.

The entrance of the sportsmen and women must be separate. Arrangement should also be made for the entrance of ambulance and fire engines if the need arises.

Waste paper baskets should also be placed at suitable places to keep the stadium clean.

HANDLING THE EXTERIOR TRAFFIC

If arrangement is made to enable the outflow of spectators in a short time but there is not sufficient arrangement for the public transport system and for its movement in a reasonable time, the purpose will not be served. The two systems are very much linked with each other and these should be properly balanced.

The tickets have to be checked properly before the spectators are allowed to enter the stadium. So it should be so arranged that the visitors enter the stadium one by one.

On the other hand the outlets should be as wide as possible. The gates should open in the outside direction. These should be in larger number and located so as to allow the spectators to make exit in all directions particularly where the public transport system is available.

There should be larger area behind the outlets to enable the visitors to leave without any difficulty.

The visitors to the stadium either come on foot, bicycles, scooters, cars, and buses. Sometimes they come by rail, trams or underground railway. The position varies from town to town. As buses are capable of conveying public in large number as much use as possible of this means of transport should be made. Bicycles, scooters and cars add to a little confusion.

It is necessary to make separate arrangements for the parking of bicycles, scooters, cars and buses. It is approximately known how many public or private buses are likely to arrive. Some estimate of cars and scooters can also be made on the basis of the number of these vehicles registered in the town.

On the basis of the number of these vehicles and the space required for each such vehicle, the parking areas for these vehicles can be calculated. Some extra area may be added to these calculations to cope with extra traffic and for maneuvering of the vehicles.

The space for cars can be best utilized if these are parked as shown in the figure below.

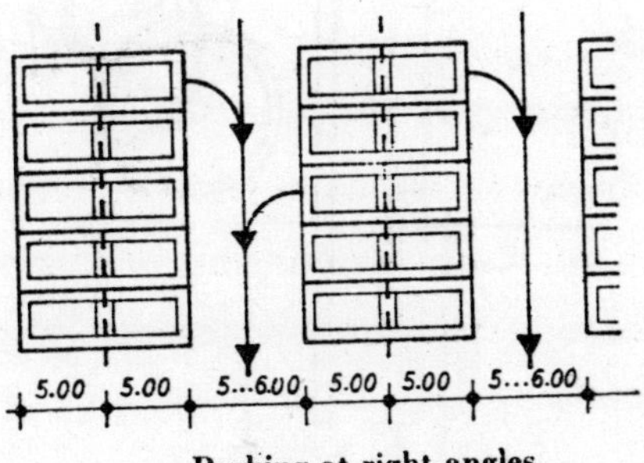

Parking at right angles

The parking of cars obliquely as show in the figure below facilitates quick departure but it requires more space and this is advisable if enough parking area is available.

Stands for bicycles should be close to the stadium. If possible, the safety of the bicycles against theft should be ensured by securing them to the stands. Stand with wheels propped up can also be provided. These stands are usually arranged in two rows as shown in figure below.

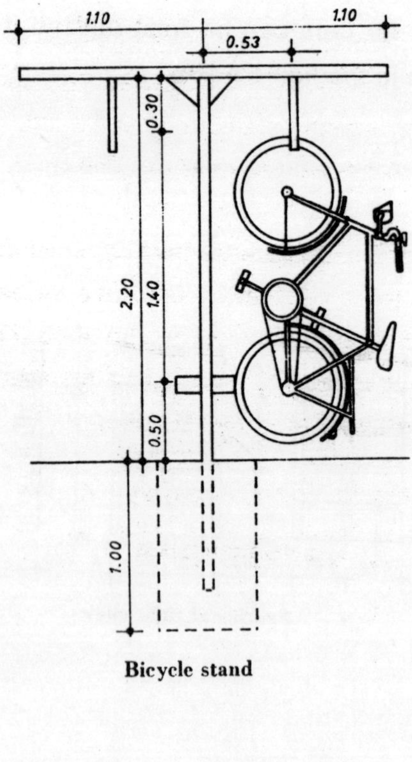

Bicycle stand

Normally, a space of 50 m^2 is required for parking buses and lorries, about 15 m^2 for parking of a motor car, about 2 m^2 for parking a motor cycle and about 5 m long space for parking 10 cycles.

In order to avoid confusion, the ticket-office and entrance should be at some distance from each other. The tickets should be of different colours and shapes to facilitate their distribution. The ticket-office should have a telephone. If there is likely to be rush at the ticket-office, provision of some benches should be made for use of waiting visitors.

A police station should also be provided. Fire-brigade and ambulance should be located near the entrance to facilitate their entry into the stadium if need arises. The police station should also be located near the entrance.

The stadium should be attractive. Special attention for this purpose has to be paid to the entrance. Green group of trees and flags of different colours can be used. Figure work, painting and other means of decorative art that affect the people of that particular area can be used.

CHAPTER-29

GROUND STANDS

Ground stands which normally have a roof are also provided. These are in addition to the tiers. These are of different sizes and designs and are made of steel or reinforced concrete.

Sometimes, there is great rush to the stadium and the seats or standing room provided may become insufficient. To meet the extra requirement, dismountable stands of steel tube may be added. It should be possible to erect them at short-notice. These are removed after the event is over.

■■■■■■■■■■

CHAPTER-30

SUPPLEMENTARY INSTALLATIONS

SUPPLEMENTARY INSTALLATIONS FOR VISITORS

It is necessary to provide water-closets, call-boxes, kiosks for the sale ot refreshment for visitors. Sometimes, this is neglected and no provision for them at the initial stage of planning is made.

WATER-CLOSETS

Water-closets should be within easy reach of the visitors. These may be close to the primary paths. Each water-closet should be provided with a small fore-room designed as a lavatory. These may be segregated by means of treesand shrubs. The water-closets and lavatories should have bright illumination and should be almost odourless and clean at any time. Water-closets for men and women should be separate. Arrangement should be made for 10 water-closets for every 1,000 women and 2 water-closets and 10 urinals for every 1,000 men.

A stationary stall may be erected at a suitable place preferably near the entrance. Movable booths can also be provided. The range of goods offered can be varied and extended. It should be ensured that goods offered are fresh.

CALL BOXES

Call-boxes with coin-pay facilities should be provided for the spectators. There should be somewhere near the entrance. One telephone for about 3,000 visitors will probably meet the requirement. In addition to the provision of telephones for the visitors, special telephone facilities will have to be provided for the press.

SUPPLEMENTARY INSTALLATIONS FOR SPORTSMEN AND WOMEN DRESSING, WASHING AND SHOWER ROOMS

Separate dressing, washing and shower rooms should be provided for sportsmen and women. Dressing rooms are combined with washing and shower rooms. As the sports person have to change their dresses at the same time, the capacity of the dressing rooms should be large enough. One dressing room is provided for about 12 persons as it is considered that a team has approx. 12 members. Large dressing rooms for large number of players say around 30 are also provided. Board with pegs and wardrobes with small boxes and locks are also provided. Each wardrobe and dressing place should have sufficient space for easy movement of the sportspersons.

Plan and side views of the dressing-rooms with benches and boards with clothes pegs, with benches and built in cupboards and with benches boxes and clothes-pegs are illustrated in the figure below.

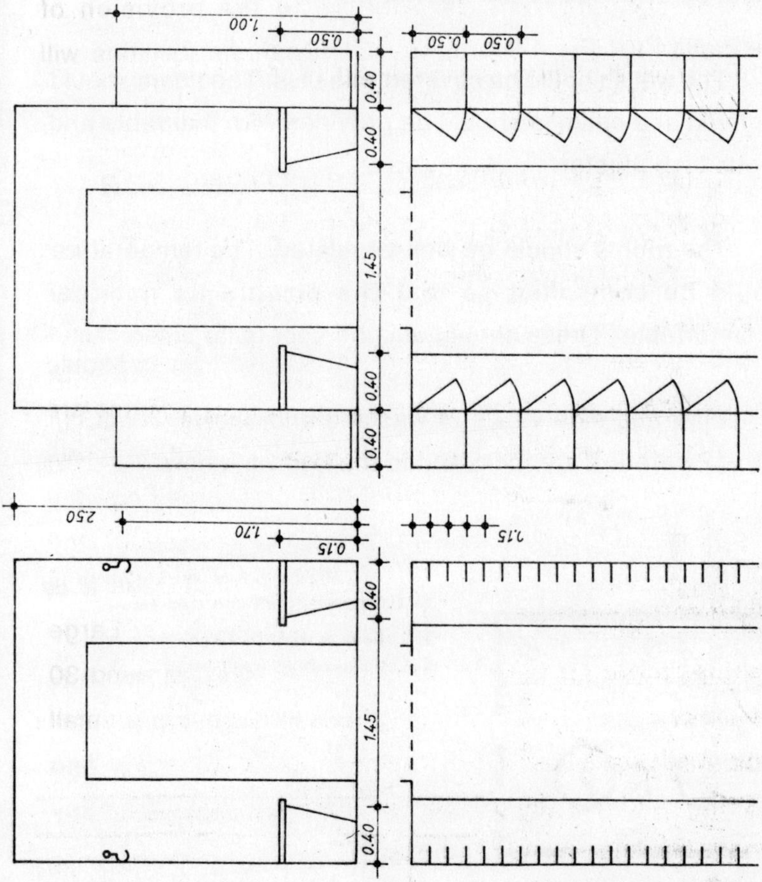

Dressing-rooms (plan and side views), left to right:
with benches and board with clothes-pegs   with benches and built-in cupboards

Warm water should preferably be available in the shower bath. As feet are spoiled in most sports, additional foot basins should be provided.

In addition to the main W.C. installations, water-closets should be attached to the shower-baths.

The walls should be covered with tiles. The floors should be paved and ceilings should be provided with a durable and porous lime plaster.

The rooms should be well-ventilated. The temperature should be controlled so that the players do not feel uncomfortable. These should also be kept quite clean.

Plan and side views of washing and shower room for 18 to 12 persons are indicated in the figures below.

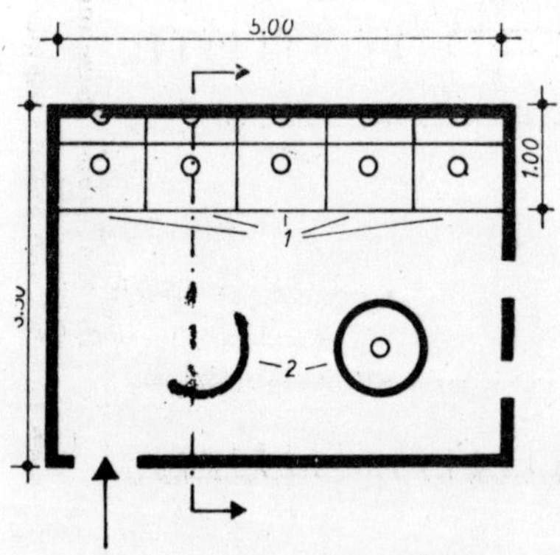

Washing and shower room for 18 to 20 persons, plan and side views

1 5 showers with footstool
2 Fountain-type wash basin

It includes 5 to 6 shower-baths with safety valves, 5 to 6 foot basins and 10 to 12 hand basins. Washing and shower-room should contain all the necessary accessories as wall hooks for towels and clothing, soap dishes, brackets for toilet-articles.

For several dressing rooms, sometimes a central shower room which has several showers is provided. A centrally-operated shower installation is used and this ensures instantaneous high-rate discharge and is economical in use.

FINISH VAPOUR BATH

A Finish Vapour both is not very expensive but is a great attraction for many people and helps them to keep in good health. It can be arranged in the basement of the dressing rooms or in a single structure close to it. It consists of a fore-room and a bath room. The dimension of the bath room is 4m x 5m. Stones are heated to increase heat in the both-room. The heating is done from the fore-room. The people lie on step type wooden frames or take a bath seat. Cold and hot showers are provided in the fore-room. For cooling down, a pool may also be provided.

WATER CLOSET

The water closet for sports persons should be adjacent to the dressing room. For dressing places for 40 men, 1 water closet and 3 urinals are required and for 40 women, 3 water closet are required in addition. These should be brightly illuminated and should be odourless and clean.

ROOMS FOR MESSAGE AND FIRST AID

For small stadium, there can be one room to meet both these requirements. The room should be quite clean, well ventilated and properly lighted. Banches should be provided for message. The room should also have equipment for first aid. To avoid any interference in treatment, the room should be in a quite part of the building. For big stadium, there can be two separate rooms for the purpose.

ROOMS FOR SPORTS INSTRUCTORS, COACHES AND REFEREES

Sport instructors and coaches should be provided a room for changing clothes etc. There should be a separate room for referees as they are not expected to share the same room with instructors and coaches of the rival teams.

ROOMS FOR THE STAFF AND IMPLEMENTS AND ORGANISING COMPETITIONS

A room should be provided to the sports field keepers and his helpers for changing clothes and for the rest.

The sports field keeper should also be provided with a workshop. It caters for small repairs. It should have the necessary tools for metal working and wood working.

Implements such as wheel barrow, buckets, brooms, shovels are required for the maintenance of fields and buildings. A separate room should be provided for them and they should not be kept together with sports equipment.

For sports equipment, there should be a separate room. These should be properly taken care of and should be arranged properly. Cabinets, racks and shelves are provided for the purpose. As these implements have to be given to the sports persons and a record has to be kept, entry in this room should be controlled by putting a table near the entrance.

A room should be located at a central place to collect the result of the competition. From here necessary instructions are also issued. The telephone exchange of the interior telephone system of the stadium is located in this room. The telephone exchange is connected to the local telephone exchange.

The competition office and the officials calculating scores and results in case of small stadium are also accommodated in this room. In case of big stadium, these should be accommodated in separate rooms.

A separate room in the case of big stadium should also be provided for press information bureau.

A floor space for these rooms should be provided as is necessary in accordance with the importance of the stadium.

In case of big stadium, a flat should be provided for the stadium manager in the main building. It will ensure continuous inspections of the stadium and has many advantages.

■■■■■■■■■■

CHAPTER-31

TECHNICAL EQUIPMENT

A stadium requires power and water supply system, soil pipe systems and heating system. These requirements should be provided as in the case of any other building and there is nothing special about them.

Special technical equipment required for a stadium are telephone system, public address system and floodlight system.

TELEPHONIC SYSTEM

A telephone system of fixed installations should be provided. It should connect all the important points with the centre. The cables should be buried under the ground and the junction boxes are installed at the end of the telephone lines when the stadium is constructed. The telephone poles should be installed and wires should better be fixed at that time.

PUBLIC ADDRESS SYSTEM

The spectators and competitors have to be imparted quick information. For this purpose, an efficient public address system is installed. For an efficient system there should be proper diffusion of sound and this should be tested before the installation is fixed. The sound system varies from place to place. As sound is absorbed by the crowd, the number of visitors likely to frequent the stadium should be kept in mind. The microphone should work from a room from where a wide view of the stadium is possible. The amplifier system also works from this room.

Portable address system is arranged in case of small stadium.

FLOODLIGHT SYSTEM

Now-a-days important sports events are held during day and night.

This is staged in large stadium. The competitions are held during night because it is considered that the conditions for competition are much better in the evening.

A flood light system which can illuminate the field uniformly is required. For this purpose necessary power should be available. Whereas for slow matches a horizontal lighting intensity of 1 : 3 will suffice but for fast matches it should be 1 : 2.

The source of light should be at suitable height from the ground so that it does not dazzle the eyes of the competitors. To meet this requirement, the angle between the central axis and the source of light should be at least 20 degree.

Different lighting intensity is required for different games. It also varies in accordance with the size of the stadium, nature of the game, training or competition and fields with or without auditorium. Lighting intensities required for some of the important events are given in the table below.

Sports or game	Facility	Mean horizontal lighting intensity in lux
Football, handball, rugby, hockey	Playing field Small stadium Large-scale stadium	100 150 to 200 300 and more
Tennis	Training Competition	100 to 200 300
Basketball Volleyball		100 and more 150 to 200
Track and field athletics, running events	Training Auditorium	100 200
Tracks and field athletics, jumping and throwing events	Training Auditorium	200 300 and more

INSTALLATION OF FLOODLIGHT SYSTEMS

(A) SIMPLE SPORTS FIELD WITH TRACK

It has three towers at each longitudinal side of the track. The towers have a height of 15 m. If the field is for training only, 40 to 50 lure mean intensity will meet the requirement.

(B) MEDIUM-SIZE SPORTS GROUND WITH TIERS FOR THE AUDIENCE

It has only a few towers as shown in the table.

Audience	Number of towers	Height of towers in m	Lighting fixtures per tower	Lamps
up to 10,000	4	20	20	1,000 W
10,000 to 25,000	4	25	24	searchlight lapms
	6	25	16	

The towers should be at such a height that light source should not be in the main direction of vision of the audience. Light should not dazzle the eyes of the spectators. If the height and length of the grand stands are sufficient, light fixtures can be fitted to them.

In the case of high jumping and pole vaulting, light should be focussed in the direction of the runway, otherwise it will be difficult to see the poles distinctly. For track and field events, light should be focussed on the main event.

(C) TENNIS COURTS

Light fixtures can be suspended at stretched wires. They can also be fitted to angles or towers. Normally incandescent lamps are used.

Such lamps as that of sodium discharge lamps which discolour the human skin are not used.

The angle light fittings which are preferred are with or without anti dazzle shade. It has a movable search light ranging in light diffusion from 45 to 120 degrees.

ADDITIONAL EQUIPMENT

Certain additional equipments such as score boards, clocks, flag staff are also required. The results of the competition are recorded on the score board. It is usually erected opposite to the main grand stand. The score board may be of a simple plug type or an electronical device. A large clock should be installed to show time to the audience. Additional flag staffs should be kept to hoist flags of the nations participating in the game.

CHAPTER-32

OBSTACLE TRACKS

Obstacle Tracks are on the margin of the sports field. Turf is considered to be the best ground. The track is also used by sports persons to keep themselves fit. No specific length for these tracks has been laid down. For school children, it can be 120 m. and for adults 200 m. The height of the obstacle for school children is less than that for the adults.

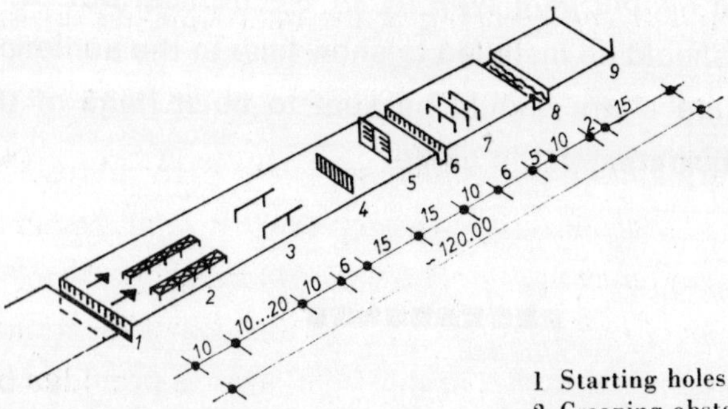

1 Starting holes
2 Creeping obstacle
3 Balance beam
4 Fence
5 Escalade wall
6 Trench
7 Triple obstacle
8 Water jump
9 Finish

CHAPTER-33

SCHOOL SPORTS FACILITIES

Now-a-days great importance is attached to physical education in schools. It is compulsory part of educational curriculum of schools. Public and private institutions prefer sportsmen in their services.

The conventional type of play ground and gymnasium do not meet the requirement. Sports facilities should be planned along with the planning of the main building for the school.

A modern school must have sufficient area to provide for proper sports facilities. It all depends on the area available to the school and size of the school. When making allotment of land for school and sanctioning a school, the educational authorities should see to it that sufficient area is provided by the school for sport facilities and that these are properly developed.

Normally an area of 30 m^2 per child should be provided for a school up to 400 children. The area can be slightly reduced for school having more children. For small school a playing field of 40 m x 60 m and an open gymnasium of 20 m x 25 m will meet the requirement. The are required will thus be 3,000 m^2.

It will be better if the sports facilities are provided at the entrance to the school. It will avoid long walks by the students. A green belt should be left between the play ground and the school building so that the studies are not disturbed.

The sports facilities are provided as indicated below.

(a) Normally the playing fields are covered with turf, borded by the sprint track. This is a large field which can also be used for small field games. The field can also be used for throwing exercise.

(b) A hard field should also be available for the rainy seasons. In areas where the weather condition is wet, the main field should also be hard and not of turf. Hard field should also be used for volleyball and handball.

(c) The open gymnasium should be adjacent to the covered gymnasium. It should have all the necessary gymnastic apparatus. Rings for marking a throwing circle can be placed into the ground or portable steel rings can be placed on the ground when required. Broad jump and high jump pits can be dug at the border of the field. The facilities for track events should be provided near the field athletics so that these could also be controlled by the sports teacher.

(d) For the play ground intended for the four lower classes, implements should not be a copy of the normal. These should be simple and connected with nature. Trees, Shrubs, Rocks and pits can be made use of.

(e) A separate though not large area should be provided for physical training and folk dance for girls of the higher classes. Trees and shrubs should be planted around this area for a little privacy to let the girls not feel any hesitation.

(f) The sprint field should have hard surface. It should have four lanes of approximately 1 m in width and 100 m in length according to the age group of the children using the field.

(g) The obstacle track should also be in accordance with age group of the children. It should be simple for small children but can be made more difficult for children of the higher classes. It should not be as difficult as for adults.

For higher classes, colleges and universities, more facilities for track and field athletics have to be provided. The facilities available in the local sports clubs can be made use of.

For some schools located near each other, a common sports ground and gymnasium can be arranged. In this case, the area required and the cost involved will be reduced.

CHAPTER-34

PLAYGROUND FOR CHILDREN

In small towns and villages, it might not be necessary to provide special playgrounds for children because there is enough space and abundant green and natural scenery available. This is not the case in urban areas. In addition to school, it is of great importance that playgrounds are available near or not at a distance from homes. Parents or elders should be able to watch the children at play from their houses or they should be able to accompany them easily to the play ground.

The playground are normally incorporated in adjacent parks. The way to the play ground should be free from traffic. There should be enough greenery, a large number of trees, bushes and good grass. Variety of flowers add charm to the playground.

The requirement of playing fields are different for different age groups as their inclinations are different as indicated in the table below.

Age group	Inclination	Basic form of playground
3 to 6 years	Playing with sand	Small place with sand pits and pool, easy to survey
7 to 12 years	Gymnastics, climbing, dynamic games	Small place with numerous implements and apparatus, lawn for playing
13 to 16 years	Ball games, athletic exercises, gymnastics	Lawn for playing on which normal sports apparatus and implements are available.

So it should be seen that the requirement of all the age groups are met. A common playground can be arranged for the first two types of children whereas separate arrangements will have to be made for the third type. This is essential as otherwise the children in the first two age groups would be disturbed or injured. It will also create. great bustle or disturbance if there is one playground for all the children.

Playground for children between 3 to 6 years does not require large area. An area of about $300m^2$ will meet the requirement.

It should include sand pit, seasaw, punch and judy show, pool for paddling, merry-go-round, swing, climbing frame, lawn, bench and playground-slide.

The pit should be filled with clean, fine grained sand which should be replaced from time to time. The pool should have a small depth so that the children of this age group can comfortably make use of it. It should have benches to enable mothers to sit on. This portion of the playground should be separated from the rest by means of thick hedges.

Playground for the next higher group age 7 to 12 years, would approximately require double of this area. They would require implements as for the children of this age group in schools. They should be provided with facilities like swings, merry go rounds, seesaw, climbing frames and playground slides. The ground should have plants and should resemble a park.

Even wrecked articles as old cars, or obsolete things are of interest to the children of this group. These can also be arranged in the playground.

The playground for children between 13 to 16 years should be somewhat similar to those provided for adults. It should provide for small groups playing at the same time as basket ball or volley ball. Pits are to be arranged for high and broad jumping and putting the shots. Climbing frame, parallel bars and horizontal bars are also to be provided.

■■■■■■■■■■

CHAPTER-35

CAMPS OF TENTS

During major sport events of national, continental or international importance, there may be paucity of accommodation for sports person as hotels might be full. So the necessity arises to accommodate the participants in tents.

If rivers, lakes or mountains are around, the tents should be located there. It can also be located where there is greenery and big trees are around to provide sunshade.

The direction of the wind must be taken in to account while pitching the tents. It should not blow into the entrance.

A good road and transport system should be available near the location of the tents. There should be proper system for supply of water.

There should be a limit to the number of tents and participants at one place otherwise there will be congestion and it will not be possible to make proper arrangements required for their lodging.

For small tents, the area required for 150 tents is & one hectare. About 400 persons can be lodged in these tents.

For bigger tents the area required is less.

Accommodation for management and kitchen should also be provided. Arrangement should be made for supply of different types of food according to the food habits of the participants.

Proper bathing facilities for men and women should be available, Facilities should also be available for washing clothes.

Latrine should not be close to the tents but at some distance. Four latrines for 100 men should be provided.

Refuse should be collected in dust bins which should be emptied daily. Arrangement should be made to keep the location quite clean and healthy. For this purpose, a few stewards should be employed. The sewage should be discharged in pits located at some distance.

Articles which are normally required by the participants should be readily available in the camp. A market for the other variety of articles that might be required by the participants should not be far away.

■■■■■■■■■■■

CHAPTER-36

Combination of Individual Sports Facilities into a well functioning whole

From practical angle, it is necessary to provide combination of sports facilities to curtail the area required for sports and expenditure, not in any way compromising with efficiency.

The large scale stadium are intended for a large number of spectators. This is not the normal requirement. Small and medium size sports facilities are very important to provide mass sports.

These are normally located in the rural areas within easy reach from a town. Sports clubs, High school or colleges use such grounds. Large areas for sports at less cost are available for sports. Large field games in addition to small games and open gymnasium are played here. These grounds are also used for strength exercise.

Special facilities such as dressing rooms, washing rooms, latrines and accommodation for maintenance staff is provided.

These facilities should be available at near the entrance. In this way, the field is not unnecessarily used and the participants find it convenient. The main sports fields should be at a distance so that the training of the individuals is not disturbed. The paths should be clearly laid down so that the participants make proper use of them and fields are not unnecessarily trampled.

A sports field can be separated from another sports field by means of hedges. There is no need to put any enclosure. Hedges are much cheap than putting up of enclosures.

The two illustrations below show the sports ground suitable for mass sports.

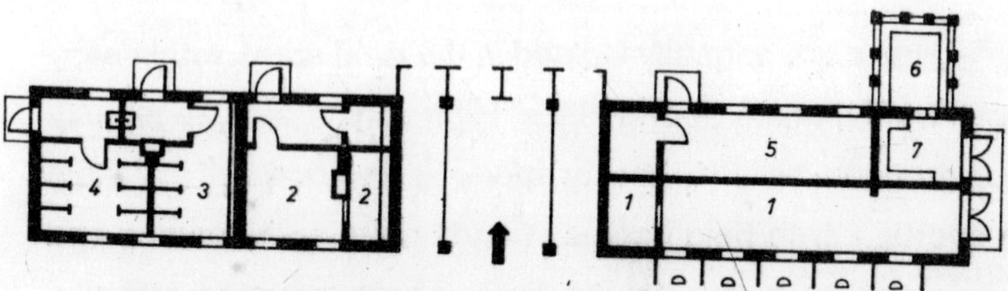

Standardised design for entrance structure with ticket-offices

1 Ticket-office
2 Head of maintenance staff
3 W.C. for men
4 W.C. for women
5 Store-room for stored implements
6 Shop
7 Store-room